SUZANNE REECE

HOW TO WRITE A 1ST CLASS ESSAY

THE EASY WAY TO PLAN, ORGANISE AND WRITE ANY ESSAY

PUBLISHED BY INSPIRED TO STUDY LTD

Also by Inspired to Study Ltd

10 Reasons You Didn't Write an Outstanding Opinion

7 Mistakes Students Don't Make in 1ST Class Dissertations.

SUZANNE REECE

HOW TO WRITE A 1ST CLASS ESSAY

THE EASY WAY TO PLAN, ORGANISE AND WRITE ANY ESSAY

PUBLISHED BY INSPIRED TO STUDY LTD

First published in Great Britain 2016

By Study Rhino Limited.

Second edition published in Great Britain 2017

By Inspired to Study Limited

Print ISBN: 978-0-9955436-7-6

Electronic ISBN: 978-0-9955436-8-3

DEDICATION

This book is dedicated to the memory of

Violet Reece.

She brought me into this world,

She protected me,

She taught me,

She loved me,

Mum

I will always love

YOU.

CONTENTS

Foreword

I first met Suzanne Reece in a professional capacity when I was reviewing her teaching sessions for the University quality assurance process. We are both professionally qualified as solicitors. I am more than delighted that Suzanne has chosen to further help students, no matter which level or subject of education they are currently pursuing.

My personal background is fully immersed in Education. I have taught and examined at nearly every level of secondary school education and beyond. At GCSE and A-level this was in modern languages; at degree level and Masters level this was in law - from law degrees, to conversion courses, to LLMs, to the professional solicitors and barristers' courses. I spent several years as director of staff training and development at one of the largest providers of legal education in the country. I have also worked as a professional body regulator of law degrees, of conversion courses and of the providers of professional assessments for solicitors. I must, therefore, have critically analysed and assessed more than a thousand fold live teaching sessions as well as quality assuring the setting of assessment essay questions and the consistency of markers of those assessments.

It was therefore with eager anticipation that I sat down to

read "How to Write a 1ST Class Essay".

If, as students, we have tried our best and worked efficiently and intelligently, it would seem only fair that not only do we pass the assessment, but that we pass it with flying colours. There are times, however, when we feel we have tried our best and worked efficiently and intelligently, yet that exceptional grade remains elusive or even worse you could discover that you have failed that assessment.

How can that be? This book answers that question for us, allowing the reader into the world of how professors and assessors think. It is extremely well structured, beginning with coaxing the reader into first creating the correct conditions in which to study. An excellent feature of this book is that it helps the reader to identify their preferred learning style and then sets out techniques which play to that preferred learning style.

The main advantage for students who read and adopt the lessons of this book, is that they will, in so doing, be producing essays which **actually answer the question.**

Far too often, in assessed essays all the way from GCSE level language essays to Masters level law dissertations, have I seen essays in which students do no more than "learn and churn" everything they have committed to memory about something mentioned in the essay question.

"How to Write a 1ST Class Essay" guides the reader through the innovative RED strategy. This equips the reader with new-found confidence that there *is* a logical approach to writing essays either at school or at college, to writing professional opinions or postgraduate dissertations. When following this approach, you can be assured that you actually have answered the question. Not only that, this is a skill that the reader can learn, apply and develop with every essay, opinion or dissertation that they write.

This book is easy to read and follow. Suzanne has highlighted and explained all the stages of writing essays in detail. The repetition and reminders that Suzanne has included keep the reader focused on the task at hand. There are recent and relatable examples covered, alongside the analogy examples which keep the reader actively engaged.

By purchasing and engaging with this book you have already started the process towards achieving that 1ST class essay. I trust that you will follow through with the skills that this book aims to help you achieve.

To hone and advance your essay writing skills still further, I recommend that you are diligent in also following Suzanne's website in conjunction with the workshops. The workshops will build on the contents of this book to provide students with hands-on guidance and with the experience of working through the necessary critical analysis of any essay question before you actually start to plan and write it and **actually answer the question!**

Gillian Woodworth
M.A., B.A.(Hons), P.G.C.E, C.P.E, Solicitor (non-practising), P.A.T.H.E, H.E.A (Fellow).
June 2017

CHAPTER 1
INTRODUCTION

"The best preparation for tomorrow is doing your best today"

— H. JACKSON BROWN JR.

HAVE YOU EVER HAD so much information you cannot work out the right answer or even what to think? Have you ever felt that you are so confused you have no idea where to start to solve that essay problem? Do you have all the academic knowledge in your head but it doesn't come out in your essays? Is it frustrating?

If you think clearly, organise your thoughts logically and write brilliant essays put this book down, you are wasting your time. If you feel you can't improve your study skills it's time to do something else, you don't need to read this book. If you DO need help organising how you think and write essays, this book is for you. Whatever your essay subjects this book will help you - keep reading.

I was a City lawyer for over 17 years and a law lecturer for nearly 10 years, teaching students how to read and evaluate case papers for professional examinations. I would sit in my office and speak to students who, having read complicated case papers, could not work out how to answer essay questions. I sat in my office one day speaking to a student, we will call her Surinder. She was a bright student but very frustrated with her performance. She had received a poor grade for a history essay.

We discussed her work and how she arrived at the decisions and answers she put in her essay. I asked her a series of questions about the essay problem. Surinder answered my questions confidently and sure of her position. At the end of our discussion her conclusions and answer to the essay question were different to those in her written essay. Surinder had all the knowledge she needed. Her problem was that she didn't understand study skills; how to ask herself the right questions and record her thoughts in a logical way.

Do you ever feel that that despite working very hard and having a good knowledge of your subject you still do not write your best essays? Do you get lost and confused by all the information in your head?

I reminded Surinder that if she followed the same system she could apply it to any subject and any essay she had to write. She thanked me for my help. As Surinder turned to leave, she asked if she could buy the book that explained this wonderful system. There was no book.

Teaching trainee solicitors and law students for over 25 years has taught me how to help students to solve problems and get those first-class grades. Years later I remembered Surinder's request and I sat down and wrote this book to help students.

What do you have to do? First, I want you to be committed to reading this book to the very end. You need to understand the complete A-Z of writing first class essays. Second, I also want you to commit to put in place the R.E.D. strategy for at least eight weeks. At the end of eight weeks you will be studying more effectively, write better essays and feel more confident with your study skills.

R.E.D. sets out our strategy for clear thinking and learning. R.E.D. stands for **R**ead, **E**valuate and **D**ecide. I need you to think of the colour red. In this book you will find the tools to help you work out problems in a logical way with examples.

Try to work through the book chapter by chapter and complete all the activities. You will learn by doing the activities, as you read because this makes your learning more memorable. We move from preparing to study, thinking about how we read, problem solving and then working on the skills you need to write your 1ST class essays. At the end of this book you will have a clear understanding why R.E.D is so important to helping you present clear arguments and answers in your essays.

The more you use the checklists and strategy the quicker you will find that you are able to evaluate information you read. You will be ready to move on to the next stage - advanced study skills and perhaps writing a dissertation. Visit **www.inspiredtostudy.org** to get further details on books, study skills workshops, private tuition and mentoring that will supercharge your learning. Also download your FREE essay planning infographics to help you plan and organise your next essay.

¶ Top Tip

Improve your study skills today
and your essays grades
will get better
tomorrow.

CHAPTER 2
ARE YOU READY?

"To keep the body in good health is a duty ...otherwise we shall not be able to keep our mind strong and clear."

– BUDDHA

ARE YOU READY? How do you feel? What is on your mind? There is no point spending hours sitting at a desk if you are not ready or able to study. I have put this chapter at the beginning of the book because it is essential that you understand why being healthy is a part of your preparation for effective study.

HOW DO YOU FEEL... TIRED OR ILL?

To study effectively you need to be physically and mentally alert. One of the main reasons students feel tired is because of insufficient sleep or because they are ill. The reality is that very few people produce first class work when they are tired or ill. When you are studying try to get at least eight hours sleep every night and avoid working long hours during the night/early morning to finish an essay. Most students are not at peak performance at 3.00am in the morning.

All colleges and universities have rules for granting extensions for essay deadlines to help students who are ill. You are not helping yourself by producing a poor essay because you are unwell; use your school or college rules to get an extension to that deadline. Applications are confidential and there is no shame in admitting that you are unwell or ill. Do the essay when you can properly focus and get a 1ST class grade.

DO YOU HAVE POOR CONCENTRATION?

Sometimes students say that they can't concentrate or they don't feel in the mood to study. How many times have you scheduled your work, sat down to start that pressing essay and just day-dreamed or wasted your time away?

The solutions are four simple steps:

SLEEP

EAT

EXERCISE

RELAX

THE 'I DON'T HAVE TIME' EXCUSE

You don't have time to eat, sleep, exercise or relax because you have an essay to write excuse. Your whole ability to think creatively is dependent on these four simple steps. When you are tired and stressed you produce your worst work because your thinking is not clear or logical. Your ability to judge the quality of your work is badly affected by a lack of sleep, lack of exercise, stress and a persistently poor diet. You can't study all the time so take time out to sleep, have a nice meal, exercise and relax.

THE POWER OF SLEEP

Have you heard of the phrase 'sleep on it'? It generally means someone wants some more time to think about a decision, usually overnight while they sleep on the problem. Research has shown that whilst sleeping the mind can find solutions and connection that the conscious mind could not make whilst awake.[1] This means your ability to form arguments, make connections and find solutions to those tough essay questions could be improved by a good night's sleep.

EAT

You cannot study properly whilst you are hungry, so eat well. This is not the time to be skipping meals. You need the energy to think and write well. If the brain does not have to worry about food it will focus on your reading and writing.

EXERCISE

You cannot spend all your time at your desk. There are serious health consequences of spending too much time sitting

---

[1] Nature 2004 Jan 22, Sleep Inspires Insight, by Wagner U,Gais S , Haider H, Verleger R and Born J

at a desk.[2] Researchers recommend breaking up sitting after 30 minutes with one to two minutes of short activity. Have a look at the recommended fitness guidelines for activity and try some of the fitness tests.[3]

Recent Research

Recent research from Stanford University found that walking helped to boost the creative thinking of people undergoing testing compared with those who were seated during the test period. For those in the test, walking outside had even better test results. The research concluded: "Walking opens up the free flow of ideas, and it is a simple and robust solution to the goals of increasing creativity and increasing physical activity."[4]

RELAX

We all have periods when stressful events happen, that is life. Find your true friends and share your concerns. Try to find a long-term fix for the problem. If the problem is too big for you to fix, talk to someone you trust. This could be a professional such as a doctor, counsellor, parent, someone from your religious community or a teacher. Just talking about a problem helps to relieve stress so imagine how good it would be to get some helpful advice and solve the problem?

All schools, colleges and universities have teachers and

---

[2] www.nhs.uk/livewell/fitness. These range from the risks associated with obesity, diabetes, cardiovascular events and some forms of cancer.

[3] http://www.nhs.uk/livewell/fitness - See for recommended activity. Try the online fitness test.

[4] Oppezzo, Marily; Schwartz, Daniel L. Journal of Experimental Psychology: Learning, Memory, and Cognition, Vol 40(4), Jul 2014, 1142-1152. (Oppezzo & L, 2014 July)

counsellors who are committed to helping you with any personal problems so reach out and get that help.

There are wellbeing classes and courses that help you find coping strategies when you feel stressed and help you understand the factors that trigger stress.

¶ Top Tip

If you SLEEP, EAT, EXERCISE and RELAX
YOU will be in the mood for studying.

NEVER feel that these are luxuries that you cannot afford, they are essential for your wellbeing.

YOU deserve
to
be
well.

I'm off
for a walk.

CHAPTER 3

HOW DO YOU PREFER TO LEARN?

YOU ARE READY TO STUDY but you need to remind yourself of how you learn. If you know how you learn you can record and present your subject knowledge in a style that suits you. If you do this, you are more likely to understand what you have read and present it in a way you and others will understand. If you can present your knowledge in a clear way you will write better essays.

ADULT LEARNING SKILLS

We do not need to go into detail about adult learning theory but it is generally accepted that adult learners have developed the following skills:

- They direct their **own study**.
- The **motivation for learning is internal** (you are in control!)
- They have **experiences** they can draw on to **help them learn**
- Learning is **driven by a need to know** (there is a problem to be solved or an essay to write!)
- They are driven to **find solutions to problems** rather than just gain information.[5]

LEARNING STYLES

Educational psychologists love to debate how learning styles develop and there are many theories. One theory is that adult students have three or four different learning styles that help them process information. During your studies, you may use more than one learning style. You will usually have a personal preference for at least one style which is related to your personality and this is called your preferred learning style. Over time it is possible your preferred learning style may change. All types of learning styles are fine.

How will you find your learning style? I will describe each learning style and you will recognise your own style; it will be obvious to you. For example, if I asked you if you like to eat chocolate, with one taste you would know the answer – it's the same with learning styles.

---

[5] Fry, H, Ketteridge, S and Marshall, S (2003) A Handbook for Teaching and Learning in Higher Education.

There are four major learning styles, easy ways of remembering them are:

VISUAL (seeing), **READING** (read & write), **HEARING** (aural), **DOING** (kinesthetic)

- **Visual learners** prefer to learn by seeing things performed, drawn or mapped out before their eyes. **'Seeing is believing' with visual learners, they remember what they have seen.**

- **Read and write learners** love reading and words. Often they are found sitting quietly reading. They like writing and often make lengthy notes. **'I have read' says the read & write learner.**

- Aural means hearing. **Hearing learners** like to learn by listening to what people say. They are busy listening but they also love talking and discussing problems so they can hear the solution. **'I hear you', says the hearing learner.**

- Kinesthetic means movement. **Kinesthetic learners** like to do things - they need movement and touch. **They learn by doing practical tasks**, building and making things. They are good at role playing. **'I made a proto-type and from that I discovered that' ...says the doing learner.**

@Activity No 1

Ask yourself – How do I prefer to learn? Tick your preferred style[s]

Remember that people have several learning styles so you

may have more than one preferred learning style.

VISUAL- [ ]

READING [ ]

HEARING [ ]

DOING [ ]

Need further help?

Still not sure which is your preferred learning style? Go to the website www.inspiredtostudy.org. You will find further information to help you understand your preferred learning style. Remember to visit www.inspiredtostudy.org to download your FREE essay planning essay planning infographics.

The advantage of using your preferred learning style

How you prefer to learn will indicate how you like to record information whilst you are studying. If you record information in your preferred learning style you are more likely to understand and retain that information. In short it makes studying easier for you.

How to use your preferred learning style

VISUAL	READ	HEARING	DOING	Add your thoughts below
SOLUTION	SOLUTION	SOLUTION	SOLUTION	
Draw pictures, diagrams or time-lines to work out essay questions -you need to see the problem.	You love every-thing printed so make sure you get a copy of the written lecture notes and all the printed slides and handouts	You listen and talk through problem solving - so find a study group and work with others who like discussions	You cannot simply sit at your desk so move around whilst you pro-cess the prob-lem. You need frequent breaks so you can move around and think.	
Visualize your-self in the prob-lem. Use visual aids such as Trello to help you chart your work. Turn words into pictures, charts or diagrams.	Write your own notes as this is how you learn. Use apps such as Evernote to keep your notes organised.	Ask questions- and listen to the answers in group learning. Talk out loud and verbalise the problem. Talk out loud to hear the solu-tions if you are on your own!	Make models of the problem and try to model the solution and then write it down. Draw a wireframe or outline the prob-lem on a story-board.	
Organise your work. It helps you to see the whole picture	Turn pictures and diagrams into words.	Listen to record-ings or webinars and lecturers. Find podcasts and listen to ra-dio debates on your topic.	Use modelling apps to see the practical prob-lem. Try Mind-Nodes, Coggle or Edraw or online apps that help with story-boards and wireframes	

VISUAL	READ	HEARING	DOING	Add your thoughts below
SOLUTION	SOLUTION	SOLUTION	SOLUTION	
Express your answer in pictures before writing your answer	Your focus is the words you like to read silently so find a quiet place to study where you can focus on words	Use computer aids that talk to you	This kind of learning is great for physical tasks – such as learning physical skills, practical sciences or computer skills.	
Use lots of colour	Use highlighters when reading to make words stand out	Join a blog or social media discussion forum	If you have a physical object – hold it, touch it and try to work out a practical solution	
Use visual aids/ flow charts /maps	Read articles or blogs rather than watching video recordings	Dictate your thoughts using computer voice recognition software	If you do not have a physical object, then role play helps - get into role and find the solution	
Use different colour highlighters when reading and writing notes - make a memorable visual statement for your mind to remember	Revision for you is to reduce your lengthy notes into shorter memorable notes. Don't be tempted to simply browse through your notes	You like discussions but most assessment at some stage will be written so do not forget to write down your thoughts	Modelling and role play are great but don't forget to write the answer down.	

How Do You Like to Present Information?

You have done a great job of recording the information in your head, the second stage is to consider how you like to present that information. This is closely related to your preferred learning style. **If you present information in a style that you prefer you are more likely to convey that information in a style that you and others will understand.**

Example

The Mathematics Haters and Lovers

I had law students who hated any form of calculations. They hated having to work out financial schedules. They would convince themselves they could not answer questions presented in this way (even with a calculator). I spent a large part of the class convincing these students that the arithmetic formulas were very simple and easy to work out. Other students loved calculations and could work out very complex legal problems in this format with great ease and apparent enjoyment! Both groups understood the law but those students who hated any form of arithmetic struggled to answer these questions. Do you like mathematics?

Use Your Preferred Presentation Style

Students often have a preferred style of presenting their information and if your assignment allows you to do this then use your preferred style of presentation. This will allow you to express your knowledge in a style that you understand and find easier to present.

For example, in group work students are often required to provide an answer on a chosen topic or problem. How they present that answer is usually in the format of a presentation to the class. Students who are confident with their spoken skills will choose to present their results in a confident spoken presentation. Other students who like writing may choose to present animated PowerPoint slides with a detailed written handout for the group.

I was told of a young student, aged seven, who was so confident with her computer coding skills that, rather than write the answer to her homework, she just coded a short computer program of a map to demonstrate her answer.

You may not have the choice of how you present your answer in an assessment but in many assignments, you have more choice than you think. Read your assignment paper carefully and check with your tutors, if you are unsure, on how your work must be presented. Use your preferred style of presentation whenever you have the choice. You are more likely to present your ideas, arguments and views more clearly if you are expressing them in your preferred style of presentation. You may have more than one preferred presentation style. Think about it.

How Do I Find My Preferred Presentation Style?

@ ACTIVITY NO 2

Ask yourself: do I like to:

- **speak** and present to a group? [ ]
- **write** out my answers in notes and give the group a detailed handout? [ ]
- produce an **audio or podcast** for others to listen to? [ ]

- produce a **model or demonstration** to explain the answer to the problem? [ ]
- draw **diagrams, map or graphs** to explain the answer to the problem? [ ]
- produce a **computer** program, **animation or video** to explain the answer to the problem? [ ]
- **write essays** on interesting topics for group discussions? [ ]

Tick your preferred presentation style(s).

You are ready, you have found your preferred learning style and you know how you learn. There is just one more thing to organise before you get into the R.E.D. learning zone. We will look at your study environment as the final preparation for studying in the next chapter.

¶ TOP TIP

If you know how you **prefer to learn**
You will **retain the information** you learn.

If you know how you **prefer to present** information
You will **present in a way you and others will understand.**

I'm a doing learner, what is your learning style?

CHAPTER 4

GET READY TO READ

GET READY TO READ. Everyone thinks that you just start reading but if you do not have the right environment your reading and thinking will be poor and interrupted. Disruptive reading is less effective than focused reading. In this chapter we will look at how to get ready to read in a productive way. Your objective is to make it easy for you to focus on reading.

COLLECT YOUR TOOLS

Start by collecting together in one place all your reading material, books, articles, open webpages, templates, calculators or other online resources. Once you start reading you do not want to break your R.E.D. time by having to go and collect or find other materials.

ADJUST YOUR ENVIRONMENT

Your study area is important it should be **quiet** to allow you to focus. It should be **bright** so you can read easily. The temperature of the room and your chair should be **comfortable** for you. There must be sufficient **space** for your papers, laptop and anything else you need. Whether you choose a library, your bedroom or a study room it must have these four elements:

- quiet
- bright
- comfortable
- space

Erase All Distractions

Your next task is to erase all distractions. Turn your phone to mute (forget vibrating that is still distracting!), turn off the TV, close your social media pages and turn off your music! I hear you protesting that your music helps you think better. There may be an important call or your friends might want to send you a message; forget it - this is study time. Does an athlete, footballer or racing driver take calls when they are out training? I don't think so and neither will you. This is the time to focus on your reading.

Types of Reading

Let's start by recapping on the different types of reading:

1. **Superficial reading** - Here you just cover the basic outline so you may only read a couple of lines or paragraphs to understand the broad outline. This type of reading often involves skipping over a lot of detailed information. This type of reading is very fast but you don't read the detail.

2. **Double reading** - Here you read something superficially to get the basic outline and then you go back and read it again. For example, you typically use this style when reading long essay questions. This type of reading starts fast but slows down when you re-read the work. You may make notes on the second reading.

3. **Detailed reading** - Here you read every word and paragraph carefully and make a record as you read. This is a slow reading pace but typically you only read the work once and have a very detailed understanding of what you have read.

R.E.D. Reading

Superficial reading is fine if you are reading a menu at your favorite restaurant or take away café but it does not work for R.E.D learning. **You cannot properly read, evaluate and decide if you have not processed all the information; so double reading or detailed reading is required for R.E.D.**

R.E.D. requires 'active reading', this does not mean that you do press-ups as you read but your mind must be focused on the reading. How many times have you sat at your desk reading something only to find that five minutes later you have no idea what you just read? **The best way to actively read is by making some sort of record that reflects your learning style.** You choose how you want to record information. It may be a flow-chart, picture, grid-table, a list, voice recording or a written note. Simply reading without any form of record taking is the best way to fall asleep!

TIME ESTIMATE
(THE QUICK GUESS)

You need to make sure that you have enough time to complete the task you have set out to do. This requires you to guess how long the whole task will take and to check that you have enough time. This does not require complicated arithmetic, just guess how long you think it will take and add an extra 30 minutes to be on the safe side. Do you find that your essays always take longer than you think?

If you hate details skip the next paragraph but remember to look at Appendix B when you finish the book. If you like detail and want to work out an accurate time-estimate have a look at Appendix B now. When you are familiar with R.E.D. learning I recommend you use the detailed time estimate approach each time you write an essay.

Now you are ready, you are in the right physical and mental state. Your environment is comfortable and you have collected all your study materials around you ready to start work. You have estimated how long the essay will take at each stage and have the time to do the work. You are prepared to get started on that essay.

¶ Top Tip

Preparation, Preparation, Preparation –

Fail to prepare
and
prepare
to
fail

CHAPTER 5

R IS FOR READING

IN THIS CHAPTER we look at how to find what you need in your reading material. You will work out how to find the key facts. You also need to be able to identify when you are missing key information. Missing information often means that you are missing key facts and we will discuss what to do when this happens. Sounds like a lot of work, so let's get started.

HOW TO FIND WHAT YOU NEED IN YOUR READING?

You do not need all the information you read. Some information is helpful background information, some is key to understanding the problem, some information has no purpose - it is just repetition or irrelevant to your essay. You find what you need in your reading by applying a few R.E.D. reading rules.

#RULE 1 – READ THE QUESTION.

What Am I Asked to Do?

Read the question or problem you have been asked to solve. READ the question or problem AGAIN and this time read every word. Look at the key words that convey the task you have been asked to complete. Are you being asked to explain, discuss, describe, advise or assess?

@ACTIVITY NO 3

Do the words below all mean the same thing? Use your dictionary to look up and record the meaning of each word.

Explain ....

Discuss..

Describe...

Advise ....

Assess ....

Compare...

Evaluate...

Contrast...

Distinguish ....

Summarise ....

The words above are asking you to do different tasks. Get

them wrong and you are not accurately answering the question.

What Questions Should I Ask When Reading My Essay Question?

Ask yourself the following questions:

1. What am I asked to do?

2. What is the main subject or subjects?

3. Does the task relate to a person, event, process, experiment or formula?

The Problem with Not Reading the Question Properly

So many students fail to read the question and as a result only answer part of the question. The effect is that their grades are limited to the part of the question they answered. **To get full marks you must answer every part of the question. Identify each part of the question and record it in a list or some other method that suits your learning style.**

A great way of improving how you read questions is to look at past exam papers. The more essay questions you practice, the quicker you will work out what the essay question is asking you to do. Reading past essay questions is also a good revision tool to prepare for formal exams or assessments.

#RULE 2 – FIND THE KEY FACTS

I thought I knew what facts were until I tried to describe them but I am sure you know what facts are? **A fact is '...a**

thing that is known or proved to be true.'[6] Well, is that clear? Who proves that a fact is true or known? What happens if different people believe different facts? Facts are slippery but it is your job to get hold of them. You must work out:-

- what facts are important,
- what they mean,
- where they came from.

Facts are essential for building your essay

An easy way of understanding facts is to picture the way you built a toy house as a child with toy bricks. You started with small building bricks or blocks which you stacked up to build a house. These small bricks or blocks are like our **facts - they are small bits of information** that you use to build much more complex structures. In the case of your essay, **facts are what you use to build complex arguments, theories and put forward opinions and conclusions.** You hope that this work will show that you have understood your subject and will persuade your tutors to give you a first-class grade.

Build a House or Tell a Story Method

Build a house (method)

Continuing with our building comparison when you build a house there are different functions for the building blocks.

---

[6] Oxforddictionaries.com

Some blocks are essential for erecting the house and for it to be stable. A floor, walls, windows and a roof, these are essential for a building. There are other building blocks that that just add decoration. These blocks, for example, may just decorate the windows, doors or the entrance but they are not essential for the building to be stable.

The key facts in your essay are like the essential building blocks for the house. Without the key facts the arguments, theories and conclusions in your essay will not fit together or work. These are the main facts on which all other arguments, theories and conclusions are based. You will usually find them at the beginning of your reading material before the more complicated discussions. Like the house, with the solid floor you will see these as soon as you walk into the house. In the "build a house method" you will find the key facts in the early parts of your reading material.

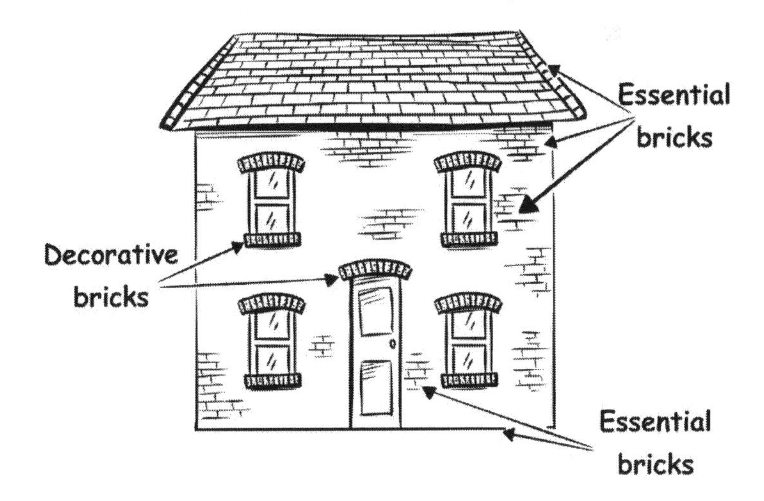

Tell a story (method)

Another way to find key facts is with the 'tell a story method'. A story starts at the beginning with the information that sets the scene and provides background information. The story progresses and more important information is added to the story until you get to the essential point of the story. Here, where you get to the whole point of the story are the essential or key facts. The facts that are key to the story are not at the very beginning but buried in the middle of the story.

Unlike the "build a house method" where we start with the key facts, in "tell a story method" the key facts are in the middle of the story. They are not apparent at the beginning and you must read some way into your study material before it is clear where the key facts are.

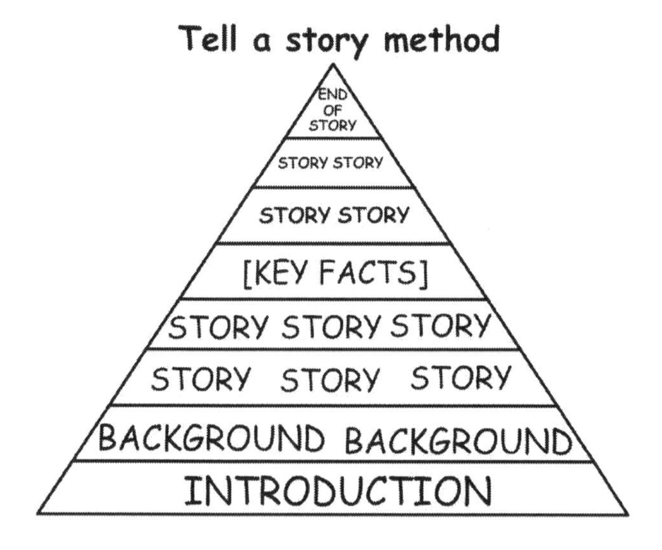

Your job is to work out what kind of structure ("build a house" or "tell a story method") you have in your study material - are the key facts up front at the beginning like the structure for the house or buried in the middle like a story? You must find the key facts.

HOW WILL YOU KNOW WHAT IS A KEY FACT?

Some students cannot work out what facts are important, which facts are just background facts and which facts are irrelevant. These students read their study material and all the facts seem to be important. These students instead of picking out the important or key facts simply repeat or record everything they have read. One of my students, let's call him Stephen, put it like this - 'How do I know what facts I am looking for. When I am reading everything seems important?'

This condition is called 'I can't see the wood for the trees' it means everything looks the same and I can't see the most obvious thing in front of me. Sometimes you are looking at the detail and cannot see the bigger picture. You get so focused on the detail you miss the obvious. For example, you see the individual trees in the wood but don't spot that together they make up the forest.

What Questions Help You Find the Key Facts?

The facts that are important will depend on the problem or question that you are trying to solve. Go back to your reading material and ask yourself the 5 W's questions:

- **What** happened?
- **When**?
- **Where**?
- **Why**? – questions - why did it happen? why that theory? why did that result occur?
- **Who?** - questions – Who was there? Who said that…? Who was first…?

If you can answer the 5 W's questions you will find the important or key facts in your reading material.

WHAT HAPPENS WHEN KEY FACTS OR INFORMATION IS MISSING?

#RULE 3

FIND THE GAPS IN YOUR FACTS

You have found the key facts in your reading material but sometimes important facts or information is missing. If key facts or information is missing, then you only have part of the story. If you only have part of the story this will make the task of evaluating what you have read more difficult. If you cannot find the missing facts or information you need to take this into account when evaluating what you have read.

How Will I Know If There Are Important Missing Facts and Information?

Remember you are NOT looking for all gaps or missing information, you just need to spot the important missing facts and information. If the missing facts or information are minor or unimportant to understanding the 5 W's (what happened, when, where, why, who) that is ok - sometimes there is always some minor information that you don't have.

HOW TO FIND GAPS OR MISSING FACTS?

a) Look at the facts you have.

It is important for you to make a record of the key facts you have. Look at them.

b) Think like a detective

There is no secret formula - just trust your instinct to spot a problem. Try to put yourself in the shoes of the person telling the story, who has written the book or article or is presenting the data. Think about the facts you have and ask yourself: if I were a detective or in the secret service what other facts or information:

- **should I have** for a complete understanding of the problem or decision?
- would I **expect** to be given to me?
- **would I have told** if this was my story?
- What other facts would my **Mum, Dad or another family member ask for** if she/he were on this case?

c) Think like yourself

- What information is missing from the facts I have read?
- What further information should I have?
- Why is it missing?
- Where should I look for more facts?
- Who will know where to find the additional information?
- Where is the document or person referred to by someone else?
- Does someone refer to another book, report, article or person? Do you need to read or see this?

Why You Need to Find the Missing Facts or Information

If you can identify that there are **important facts and information missing** you should be able to **describe** what fact or information is missing. If you know what fact or information is missing you may be able to **work out where to find the missing information**. If you find the missing information then you have all the facts and information to come to **clear decisions** and **conclusions in your essay**.

Try this:

- **Identify** there is a missing fact or information.
- **Describe** the missing fact or information.
- **Decide where to look** for the missing fact or information.
  (Do you have to read another book, report, statement or statistics?)
- **Find** the missing fact or information.

If You Can't Find the Missing Facts or Information

If you can't find the missing facts or information you will need to make it clear that your view, assessment or opinion is limited to the information you have read.

Example

In our house building example, I have built this house and tested everything except the loft room. You tell the owner 'be careful going into the loft, I have not been able to find the loft ladder to test that the electrics are working up there'. You have explained the limits of your answer: I have tested everything except the loft and explained why.

You would take a similar approach with your essay conclusions. This means that you present your conclusions but they will need to be reviewed in the future; when further facts or information is obtained. This is a provisional conclusion based on the facts and information you have now.

The advantage of this approach is that your tutor will recognise that you have spotted that IMPORTANT facts or information are missing. You should get extra marks for spotting that something was missing AND still being able to decide and conclude on the essay topic even if it is a provisional conclusion.

¶ TOP TIP

Facts are everywhere
your job is to spot the
important
Facts!

CHAPTER 6

FIND THE KEY TOPICS OR PROBLEMS

YOU HAVE IDENTIFIED THE FACTS but that is only part of the story. You now need to identify the key topics or problems as this will help you to answer the question or test you have been set. We will discuss how you find the key topics or problems in this chapter.

LOOKING FOR THE KEY PROBLEMS

#RULE 4
FIND THE KEY TOPICS OR PROBLEMS

The key facts should help you to identify the key topics or problems to be resolved in your essay. The **key topics or problems will depend on the question you have been set.**

Go back to your question and look at what you have been asked to do, remember how you recorded the key words in the question, well it is time to focus on this again.

What you are looking for is the broad topic or problem, if you had to describe the problem in one or two sentences how would you describe the problem? The more complicated the essay question will mean there are several topics or problems that you need to resolve in answering the essay question. Your task here is to list all the topics or problems. At this stage do not worry about putting them into any specific order just find them.

Now you know how to spot the key problems or topics it is time to move to the next stage; how to find and separate out different arguments and opinions. Time to introduce a new rule.

RULE #5 FIND AND SEPARATE THE MAIN ARGUMENTS.

Reading Academic Discussions in Your Study Materials

The main feature of academic work is that there are always several different arguments for and against a position, theory or opinion. The arguments in support and against a particular position will need to be discussed in your essay. Just to make things more difficult authors will often combine, compare and discuss more than one argument, theory, position or opinion in the same paragraph, as they believe this demonstrates complex thinking and great intellectual ability.

I have found 3 key problems,
are there any more?

Don't panic, just think of this as a plate of Italian spaghetti, how would you go about trying to eat this?

FIND AND SEPARATE EACH MAIN ARGUMENT

Before you start to discuss different arguments, you need to **find and understand each main argument, theory or opinion relevant to your essay.** Think of this as the stage where you sort out the mixed-up spaghetti on your plate. First, careful reading of your study material should help you to identify the different arguments. Use the same approach as you used for spotting the different topics or problems in the last chapter. Your job is to unwrap these arguments or discussions, so that you can separate each argument before you can begin to take a more detailed look at them and compare them with each other.

HOW TO DEAL WITH DIFFERENT POSITIONS

This is also known as the how to eat spaghetti method. The way you tackle the different positions, theories, opinions or data in your reading materials is by following a simple formula, it works every time.

- **Give each argument a separate name.**
  Start by finding each argument and giving it a separate name.

- **Make a record of the argument.**
  Make sure that whilst reading you record (in a style that suits your preferred learning style) the essential parts of the position, argument, theory or opinion.

- **Only compare similar arguments on the same topic or problem.**
  You should only compare similar theories or arguments on the same subject, topic or problem.

- **How is each argument similar to the other arguments?**
  Now it is time to compare the different arguments. Record where they agree.

- **How is each argument different from the other arguments?**
  Now it is time to find the differences in the arguments. Record where one argument puts forward a position and the other is different or silent on the same point.

- **Check out the information, evidence or data each argument is based on.**
  Record what data, information or evidence each argument is based on. Are both arguments based on the same facts or data?

One argument may be based on different or newer data than another, you need to take this into account when comparing your arguments. Newer research data with larger test groups (cohorts) combined with modern research tools may mean later data is more accurate and reliable than older data. Don't however assume that old is always out of date sometimes newer research tools prove that old theories are in fact true!

Spend Some Time Thinking

You will have to spend time thinking about the information you have recorded. This is perfectly normal - take time to think things through and see, hear and find the big picture. Look at the big picture- how do the arguments fit together overall in your essay? Does one or more argument provide a better answer to the essay question?

Your Objective

At the end of this process you should:

- clearly **understand** each academic argument.
- You should be able to **summarise the main arguments** in a few sentences
  Say it out loud: does it make sense?
- You should also be able to show how the different positions, arguments, theories, opinions, or data are **similar and different from each other.**
- You should have a clear understanding of **how they contribute to answering the essay question.**

SUMMARY

You have done a lot in the last couple of chapters, so let's just recap. You have started reading and identifying the key facts. You have identified the key topics or problems for debate in your essay. You found and understood the key arguments, how they compare and are different.

If you can identify the key topic or problem, it will help you to focus on understanding the different positions, arguments, theories, opinions or data in your reading material. Once you separate the different arguments, you will be able to compare them and see why and where they are different.

You are doing more than simply repeating information you have read; you are analysing the information. These rules provide you with essential skills for writing first class essays and getting the higher marks because they demonstrate intellectual ability. You are well on the way to critical thinking!

Congratulations on completing the 5 rules of reading.

THE 5 RULES OF READING

RULE 1 – READ the question

RULE 2 – FIND the KEY FACTS

RULE 3 – FIND the GAPS in the FACTS

RULE 4 – FIND the KEY TOPIC or PROBLEMS

RULE 5 – FIND & SEPARATE the main ARGUMENTS.

¶ TOP TIP

Sorting out your mixed up spaghetti always makes it easier to eat!

CHAPTER 7
E IS FOR EVALUATION – THE BASICS

E IS FOR EVALUATION. Some students think this is the hardest part of the R.E.D. learning but if you have done your reading correctly this will be easy. In this chapter you will work out how to evaluate or assess the facts and information you have collected so you can work out the arguments and opinions you will use in your essay. The key is to follow each stage of the evaluation formula without missing out any steps.

HOW DO YOU BUILD AN ESSAY ANSWER?

If you can understand how you build an essay answer it is much easier to understand what you need to put into that essay. You start with reading and from that you identify the key facts which help you understand the key topics or problems. You use the key facts which are supported by other information (for example, data, research, case-law, laws, documents, recordings, witnesses etc.) to start to develop theories and arguments. Your arguments and theories help you develop conclusions. Your conclusions form the basis of your answer to the essay question.

EVALUATION IS ABOUT FINDING THE CORRECT RANGE OF ANSWERS

One word of warning: evaluation is NOT like working out a scientific formula. Students are often concerned that they find the one right answer. What you should understand is that in more advanced essays **there is a range of correct answers.**

I often explained to my law students that tutors were not simply testing their memory or their ability to repeat facts. The purpose of assessing students' essays is to test how students have assessed the facts, supporting information and evidence. We want to see how students deal with the essay problem, form opinions, justified arguments and come to conclusions on the essay subject. Tutors want to see how students assess and critically evaluate all the information they have. The key to remember is it is NOT just about the final answer but how you have arrived at this answer that is being assessed in most subjects.

TRY THE PLAYING FIELD APPROACH

The big secret is that tutors are not looking for one single correct answer. There is a range of correct answers and you can persuade your tutor, by great arguments in your essay that your answer is in the right range of correct answers. If your answer is in the right area you can get first class marks.

Try to think of this problem as if it was a playing field for any sport. Let's divide the field into three sections and give each third of the field a colour. The red zone is the area with the wrong answers, you need to avoid this zone. Hit any of the wrong answers and you automatically go into the red zone. In this zone you got some fundamental understanding of a theory, formula or argument wrong. There is no such thing as being a little bit wrong when you get an important or critical point wrong. This is the zone of failed essays.

The blue zone is mid-field. Here is where your answers are ok but some of the answers or reasoning may be weak but overall the answer is not wrong. In the blue zone you get an average pass. This tends to be where you demonstrate you understood the key points of the essay but your application, evaluation or analysis of the essay question had some flaws or may have been weak.

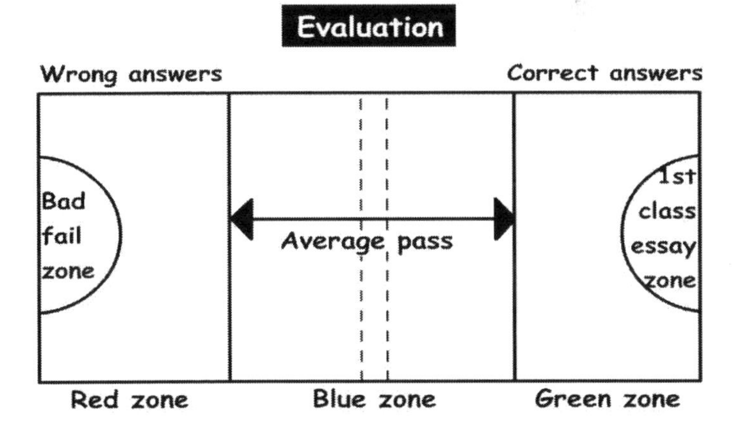

The final area is the green zone. This is the area where a range of answers are correct and you get first class marks. Your objective is to get your essay answers in the green zone. The reason there is no single right answer to an essay question is because there are a range of right answers in the green zone.

TIME TO THINK LIKE A PROFESSOR

In the evaluation stage you are going to make decisions and judgements about the facts, opinions, data, research and supporting information you have collected in the reading stage. In the evaluation stage you will need to think like a professor, judge or referee but NOT like some students.

How Do Professors Think?

Professors try to look at the facts and information from different sides. Let me explain. A judge must listen to the arguments put forward by both sides and then he must look at the arguments from the position of the judge - fairly, impartially and independently. The referee in any game takes the same approach. The referee listens to the appeals made by both sides and then considers what he/she has heard or seen. They decide by applying the rules of the game to the play. If the referee has help from technology, they use this to help them decide. In tennis, the umpire uses 'hawk eye', an electronic replay of the tennis ball bouncing near the play line to decide whether the ball was in or out. In international cricket matches the on-field umpires can refer close decisions to the off-field third umpire who has the benefit of a slow action replay of the key point.

Professors will take adopt a similar plan in considering difficult academic or research issues. He/she will identify the problem, consider the existing arguments, carry out research, evaluate the data and produce reasoned arguments and conclusions. Your job is to think like a professor.

Don't Think Like Some Students

How do some students think? Well they start with all the information they have gathered and they just want to write it down in an essay as quickly as possible. They do not have time to think or assess what they have read.

They usually make a quick decision about the right answer either before or during writing their essay. These students sometimes work out they don't like their arguments whilst writing their essay and change their conclusions as they go along. Some students never come to any decision about the answer to the essay question. They always finish their essay but often their essays fail or get a poor grade because they:

- Simply repeated what they read,
- Didn't evaluate the arguments,
- Didn't have any structure,
- Didn't have any conclusions,
- Didn't find the correct range of answers,
- Didn't answer the essay question.

THE GROUND RULES – 5 ASSUMPTIONS

Now that you understand the mindset you need let's start with some ground rules. We start with the FIVE assumptions which are the foundation of critical thinking in the evaluation stage. **Remember your aim in writing your essay is**

to find what is RIGHT, CORRECT or TRUE in your reading material. The 5 assumptions make you challenge what you read, see, do or hear.

THE FIVE ASSUMPTIONS

1. **Don't accept everything you read, see, hear or do as right, correct or true.**

2. **Every author reflects his/her own values.** Every author has their own personal beliefs, background, opinions, experiences and politics which make up their values. Their work is an expression and reflection of their values.

3. **Publication doesn't mean it's right correct or true.** Just because an author has published facts or an opinion in a book, online, in the media, produced a report or published statistics does NOT mean they are right, correct or true.

4. **YOU have the RIGHT to agree or disagree with any FACT or OPINION** but you **MUST EXPLAIN WHY**.

5. **Your explanation should be LOGICAL.** You will provide a clear, sound, reasoned explanation for your opinion.

You Have Control

This is your opportunity to judge or assess the quality or value of the information you have collected. You will decide what worth, standard or weight is to be given to the facts, arguments, formulae or data that you have read.

This is the part of your essay that will separate you from other students and get you your 1ST class grade. How you think and evaluate is the whole reason you spent so much time reading and understanding your research and study material. This is the time to think like a professor.

Don't Sit on The Fence

Imagine sitting on a fence, you are not on either side of the fence just perched awkwardly on top. Some students feel overwhelmed by the task of having to decide what worth, standard or weight is to be given to the facts, arguments, formulae or data they have read. They feel that they don't have enough experience or simply don't know enough about the subject to judge what they have read. They are wrong, go back to our five assumptions on evaluation and read them again. You will be required to get off the fence and decide which side you are on.

The 50:50 Student

Ok so we have dealt with students who don't like to make decisions but other students devise another solution to the problem which is just as bad. These students fear making the wrong decision so they always take the middle ground, they think this is the safest position. These students think that if they always stay in the middle then they have at least a 50:50 (50%) chance of getting the right answer as opposed to a 100% chance of getting it wrong, if they pick the wrong answer. They are not confident of getting the right range of answers so they make the calculation and bet in the middle.

These essay answers often sound weak in their conclusions

because they have failed to evaluate the strength and weaknesses of the arguments.

Example

A typical 50:50 essay student answer would sound like this: "...there are good arguments for A... There are equally strong arguments for B... In conclusion both sides have valid arguments ..." How do you feel reading that conclusion? What effect do you think this type of essay will have on a tutor?

Both the 'sitting on the fence' and '50:50' strategies have the same results - they do not fool the tutor. All you are saying is: "I don't know how to evaluate or assess what I have read. I don't know how to come to conclusions on what I have read. I don't want to make a decision because I am frightened I will get the wrong answer." These students may get a bare pass but they are never going to get a 1ST class grade.

Start taking control, have confidence and start making decisions about what you have read. Just take a 360 degree look around and form a view based on what you have read. In the next chapter I will help you start the evaluation process but it is up to you to start making big decisions.

¶ TOP TIP

Think like a professor,
Think like a referee,
Think like a judge.

CHAPTER 8

EVALUATION – THE PROCESS

WE DEALT WITH THE BASICS of evaluation in chapter seven now we are going to look at the mindset you require for proper evaluation. In other words, how you get into the zone for clear and logical analysis of all the information you have read. Think of this as the start of your mind training work out, having done a warm up. There are five stages to evaluation. In this chapter, we are going to look at checking your facts are correct and finding other information that supports those facts.

THE 5 STAGES OF EVALUATION

The five stages of evaluation are:

1. Check **your key facts are correct**

2. Find **other information to support** your key facts

3. Grade your main arguments

4. Find the gaps in the main arguments

5. Put your arguments in order

A. Check Your Key Facts Are Correct.

Make sure that you have made an accurate record of the key facts. It is important to state the key facts correctly. You lose marks if the facts are mis-stated, over-stated or inaccurate. Facts are the foundation of the arguments and theories you will build for your essay: get the facts wrong and you may end up with the wrong answer.

B. Find Other Information That Supports Your Key Facts

You will need to find other information that supports or confirms the key facts as being 'accurate, correct or true'. Facts can also be corroborated by other information such as official records, verified data, verified research, documents, audio or image recordings - the list can be very long.

The general rule is that facts that are confirmed by independent or official records or data are less likely to be wrong. If you can support your facts with independent or official records or data, then the theories and arguments you make, based on those facts, are more likely to convince your tutor that they are accurate, correct or true.

When you cannot find supporting information for your key facts then these essays move more towards theory and speculation. They have less influence than theories and arguments that are supported by independent and official records and data. You must work harder to convince the reader with your logic and reasoning that unsupported theories and speculation are right. The task is not impossible but it is harder.

This task should be distinguished from fake news which is facts and information which are simply made up to support a point of view or argument. Here the "so call facts" are easily found to be false when checked with independent and official records. There is often no or unreliable supporting information. Rather than framing their work as theory, discussion or speculation fake news tries to pretend that it is well researched facts and information.

C. Work Out the Quality of the Information You Have - Give It a Grade

Remember how to build your essay answer?

You start by identifying the key facts and understanding the key topics or problems. You use the key facts which are supported by other information (for example, data, research, case-law, laws, documents, recordings, witnesses etc.) to start to develop theories and arguments. Your arguments and theories help you develop conclusions. Your conclusions form the basis of your answer to the essay question.

At this stage you will have read various arguments, theories and conclusions from your reading material on your essay topic. Here you will start to evaluate or assess the quality of the main arguments you are thinking of using for your essay answer.

Not all information has the same worth, quality or standard. To help you evaluate or judge the strength or weakness of your arguments, in the evaluation stage, it is necessary to work out the 'worth' 'quality' or 'standard' of the information you have.

Have a look at the diagram below setting out some of the typical sources of information.

Diagram Showing the Sources of Information

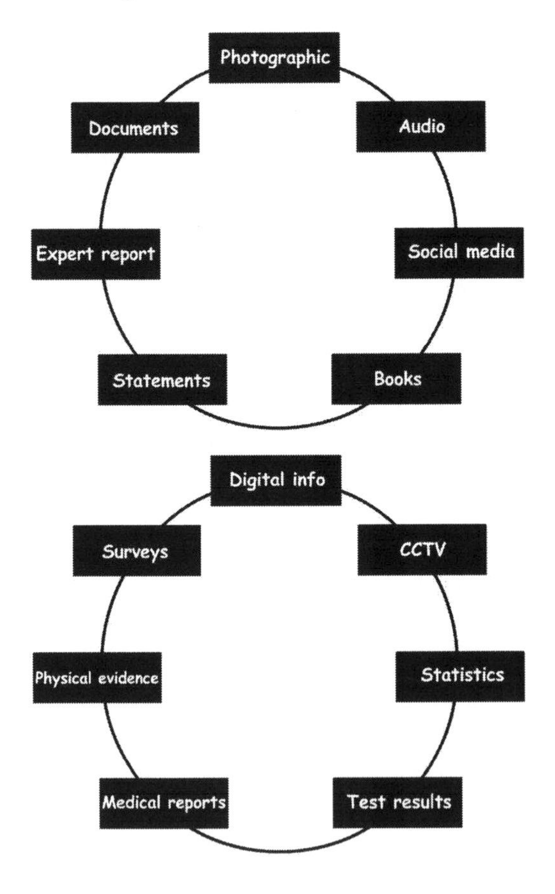

Official and independent information that has been tested, verified or corroborated has very good persuasive influence. Here think of official government records and statistics, research papers published in respected journals that have been peer reviewed and scientific experiments that have been replicated by eminent scientists. What you are trying to say with this information is, "...look at this it comes from a very good source, it has been checked and verified. You can believe this."

Make a Note of the Source of Your Main Facts and Supporting Information

To value facts and supporting information you need to record where the main information came from. Record this information as you read as you will need to review it later in the evaluation stage. This is NOT where you read the information (that goes in your footnotes and bibliography) here we are looking for something deeper: who or what specifically confirms the information as true, correct or accurate? What was the original source of the information?

Example

- You may have read a file containing three witness statements but the main statement for you is by A Hornby dated 3 February 2016. You would record the name and date of this witness statement.
- You read a series of meteorological reports but the one that is important for your essay is a specific report so you would record, for example, the meteorological report dated 4 June 2017 for the London area as the source of the key facts relating to the weather conditions on that day.

- In a commercial dispute you are asked to advise on the law. You have a copy of the lawyer's file relating to the dispute. The key document is the contract dated 21 March 2016 between Tech2000 and Smith-Palmston Plc; this is the document to record.

Let's recap: there are five stages to evaluation and you have completed two stages of evaluation.

1. **Check your key facts are correct** *
2. **Find other information to support your key facts** *
3. Grade your main arguments
4. Find the gaps in the main arguments
5. Put your arguments in order

¶ Top Tip

"Learning is a treasure that will follow its owner everywhere."

— **Chinese proverb**

CHAPTER 9
EVALUATION – HOW TO GRADE YOUR ARGUMENTS

YOU HAVE IDENTIFIED THE SOURCE of the key facts and other supporting information, now it is time to evaluate its quality.

HOW TO GRADE THE FACTS AND SUPPORTING INFORMATION

Your reading of your study material should have given you the key facts, supporting information and at least two main arguments that answer the essay question; often you will have more than two.

THE GRADING SYSTEM

Remember this is not a mathematical equation. All you are trying to do is to get your evaluation into the right range of correct answers. In the playing field approach this is getting your answer into the green zone. You can either score using numbers between one and five or a grade from very poor to very good. I prefer to use the grade approach.

Give the facts and supporting information for **each main argument a score or grade.**

Scoring system for evaluation

One = very poor

Two = poor

Three = neutral (neither poor nor good)

Four = good

Five = very good

Example

A. **Richard III,** former King of England, died in 1485 in the battle of Bosworth. In August 2012 **remains** were found in an excavation in a car park in Leicester which had been the site of a historic church. In February 2013, it was announced that scientific DNA testing of the skeleton with living ancestors confirmed that the remains were those of Richard III.

Grade this argument: very poor [ ] poor [ ] neutral [ ] good [ ] very good [ ]

B. A **prototype for a new spacecraft** has recently been announced. Information from an unnamed source said that the spacecraft will be ready for testing in the next 9 months, with the hope that customers for the spacecraft will be able to travel into space within the next 3 years.

Grade this argument: very poor [ ] poor [ ] neutral [ ] good [ ] very good [ ]

C. A **new luxury electric car** has recently been launched. Many experts in the car industry believe this stylish luxury electric car being sold at an affordable price is likely significantly to change the market. The forecast is that these cars could lead the way in a new growth in consumer spending in the car market.

Grade this argument: very poor [ ] poor [ ] neutral [ ] good [ ] very good [ ][7]

[7] Answers to above questions – facts in bold. A-very good because it is supported by scientific DNA evidence; b- poor – unnamed sources are very informal and cannot be checked (it would different if it was from a named or official source); c- Here we have the opinion of "many experts" which suggests this is a widely held view BUT you will have to do some more research to check and identify some of these experts, if this is right this would have a grade of good).

What do you do now? Nothing, just keep it as a provisional evaluation. This is not the end of the assessment, in the next chapter, you will work out if there are any gaps in your facts or supporting information.

There are five stages of evaluation and you have completed three stages.

1. **Check your key facts are correct ***
2. **Find other information to support your key facts ***
3. **Grade your main arguments ***
4. Find the gaps in the main arguments
5. Put your arguments in order

¶ TOP TIP

"The purpose of education is to replace an empty mind with an open one."

— **Malcolm Forbes**

CHAPTER 10
EVALUATION – FIND THE MISSING FACTS & INFORMATION

PART OF EVALUATING YOUR RESEARCH and reading material is to work out if there are any weaknesses or flaws with the facts, arguments and information. This usually means **finding out if some important fact or information that you need to make an argument or decision is missing.** In this chapter we will look at how to find important missing information and what to do if you cannot find it.

FIND AND EVALUATE ANY GAPS IN THE FACTS AND SUPPORTING INFORMATION

You found the gaps in the facts earlier when we looked at #RULE 3: find the gaps in the facts. Look at your record.

Now you will take this one stage further and think about the gaps in the set of facts and supporting information that make up your MAIN arguments for your essay. **For each of the main arguments you are going to test them to see if there are any gaps or missing information.**

How to Find the Gaps in the Main Arguments

Think about the facts and supporting information you have from all your different sources. Try to put yourself in the shoes of the person telling the story, pretend you are them writing the book or article or presenting the data. What have they missed out?

Ask yourself: if I were a detective what other facts or information:

- **should I have** before I decide?
- **would I expect** to be given?
- **would I have told** if this was my story?

There is no secret formula for finding something that is missing. Just trust your judgment and do not over complicate matters. Find, listen and look for the most obvious answer to the questions. Go back to the diagram on page 58 showing the sources of information; look at each source of information and ask yourself: "Should I have information from this source?"

Is the Gap in the Main Arguments Important?

You have found that something is missing - now it is time to assess how important that gap is to your essay. **You are only concerned with important gaps in the main facts and supporting information.** If the gap in the facts or supporting information is trivial or un-important you may mention it but it will not change the strength or merit of your arguments.

If the gap is important then it is time to re-evaluate those arguments. If the gap goes to one of the main problem areas you are trying to resolve in your essay, then it is important. The more important the gap in the facts or supporting information the weaker the arguments will be.

Does the Gap Weaken the Argument?

If a gap in the facts or supporting information is important it will nearly always weaken any position, argument, theory, opinion or data on which it is based. It is time to **re-evaluate your original grade for this main argument, usually by reducing the grade.** Give it a revised grade between very poor and good or a revised score between 1-4 if you are using the number method.

Scoring system for evaluation

One = very poor

Two = poor

Three = neutral (neither poor nor good)

Four = good

Five = very good

Example
A good argument may be revised to neutral or poor where an important fact or information is missing from a main argument. How far down you revise your evaluation will depend on how critical the important fact or information is to the argument.

There is further help for you. Remember www.inspiredtostudy.org provides practical tips on what to look for in trying to evaluate all the information you have. Visit www.inspiredtostudy.org to download your FREE essay planning infographics.

There are five stages of evaluation and you have completed four stages.

1. **Check your key facts are correct ***
2. **Find other information to supports your key facts ***
3. **Grade your main arguments ***
4. **Find the gaps in the main arguments ***
5. Put your arguments in order.

¶ TOP TIP

"The important thing is not to stop questioning."

— **Albert Einstein**

Chapter 11
Evaluation – Put Your Arguments in Order

You have checked your facts are correct, found supporting information that corroborates those facts, graded your main arguments and found any important gaps in your arguments. Now it is time to put your arguments in order.

Put Your Arguments in Order

Having assessed the quality of your main arguments it is now time to put the different arguments into some sort of order. **Put the arguments in order with the best arguments on top going down to the weakest arguments at the bottom.** On top are the arguments that you gave your highest grade or score.

Remember the questions you need to ask:

a) Check your key facts are correct.

b) Find other information that supports your facts.

c) Work out the quality of the information you have and give it a grade or score.

d) Are there any important gaps in the facts and supporting information? (re-evaluate your grade)

e) Put your arguments in order - put the best on top.

Spend Time Thinking

Evaluation is something that requires you to spend time THINKING, take that time. Do the thinking now and save time when you start to write your essay. Thinking now at the evaluation stage will avoid that awful feeling that you don't know what you think or how to answer your essay question when you start writing.

There are **five stages of evaluation.** Congratulations! You have completed ALL five stages.

1. **Check your key facts are correct ***

2. **Find other information to support your key facts ***

3. **Grade your main arguments ***

4. **Find the gaps in the main arguments ***

5. **Put your arguments in order ***

¶ TOP TIP

"Knowledge is power, information is liberating."

— **Kofi Annan,** Former Secretary-General of the United Nations

CHAPTER 12
MAKE THE DECISION

YOU HAVE READ AND EVALUATED the facts, supporting information and arguments and put them in order with the best arguments on top. The last stage is to sit back and congratulate yourself on a great job; well not just yet. It's time to review your work and make final decisions.

THE REVIEW

The purpose of your review is to check you have not forgotten to consider something important. Think of this stage as checking your calculations after you have worked out that complicated algebra equation. Students often think they can miss this stage out if they have been thorough in the earlier stages - don't be tempted to do this.

Often the way you see a topic or problem develop as you read more information and begin to evaluate the supporting information. As you understand the arguments being made you get better at comparing the similarities and differences between arguments. In the early stages it is easy to miss a key problem or issue when reading.

The review stage is NOT your chance to repeat the R.E.D. process but it IS TIME to do a quick CHECK. Many good essays have been turned into 1ST class essays at this stage by spotting an obvious mistake, omission or error. Go back over your notes making sure you have covered the rules:

#RULE 1 - READ the question.

Have you answered the essay question? If there is more than one question or several parts to one question, **check you have answered every part of the question.** If you want maximum marks the easiest way to do this is make sure you get marks for every part of the question.

#RULE 2 - FIND the KEY FACTS.

Did you find ALL the key facts? Check your notes that you have not missed a key fact, as this may affect your evaluation. If your review shows you have missed a key fact, then go back and work it into your evaluation.

#RULE 3 - FIND the GAPS in the FACTS.

Make sure you have found the IMPORTANT GAPS and check that you have not simply failed to read a fact. If you find information, go back and work it into your evaluation.

#RULE 4 - FIND the KEY topic or problems

These are derived from the key facts, this is thinking time so put down your pen, close your tablet or iPad and THINK. **Have you left out a key issue?** If you have go back and work it into your evaluation.

#RULE 5 - FIND and SEPARATE the main ARGUMENTS

You have sorted out **your arguments: make sure that you have them straight in your mind.** If you are clear in your thoughts, your arguments in your essay will also be clear. If you are clear on your arguments writing your essay will be much easier.

#RULE 6 - EVALUATE the facts and arguments.

Check that you have got your arguments in the correct order.

What Are Your Conclusions?

Each Topic

Try to see these conclusions on each topic or problem as a trail of stepping stones that leads the tutor from the beginning to the end of the essay. **Each topic must be discussed and at the end of each topic there should be a conclusion. Each new topic should be a stepping stone to the next topic and eventually to the final conclusion.**

Have you ever missed a stepping stone? Don't lose your tutor by missing out any of the stepping stones to your final conclusion. You will lose marks in your essay if the tutor cannot follow your arguments, reasoning and conclusion to the end of the essay.

Remember a conclusion is not your opportunity to repeat the arguments in the body of the essay. Your conclusion must be brief BUT not so brief that, having read it, the tutor is unclear why you have concluded as you have done. Conclude and put in a BRIEF explanation that justifies your conclusion.

Final Conclusion

At the end of the essay it is important to set out your final conclusion with a concise explanation of your decision. You should by now have answered the essay question.

Make Your Final Conclusion Consistent with Your Arguments

Think of this as a circle. Your arguments support your conclusions. Your conclusions rely on your arguments. Make your conclusion at the end of each topic consistent with your final conclusions. Make your final conclusion consistent with your previous arguments.

I can't tell you how many times I read students' essays where they put forward very convincing arguments in one direction only to suddenly to change direction in their final conclusion. This is a classic case of a student who changed their mind whilst writing their essay because they did not spend time thinking, evaluating and planning BEFORE they started writing.

Make an Essay Plan

One way to avoid conclusions that don't fit the arguments in the essay is to make sure you use R.E.D. and plan your essays before writing. We discuss essay planning in chapter fifteen.

Make the Final Decision

You will find that it helps to make a summary of your findings, results, theory or arguments in your essay plan. We will discuss essay plans in chapter fifteen when we look at planning your essay.

> ¶ TOP TIP
>
> You feel so much better
> when you have made DECISIONS
> and reached CONCLUSIONS
> on ALL issues

Chapter 13
Time to Add in Your Ideas

You have successfully read the facts, identified the key topics, identified the key arguments and carried out your evaluation. You have concluded on each topic or problem and reached an overall conclusion but you are not done yet. The best way to write a brilliant essay is to add in your own opinion or interpretation on the facts, data, information, opinions or theories you have read.

Time to Add Your Ideas

Ok this sounds bold; how can your views be interesting compared to those of respected academics, scientist, authors or practitioners? Well remember assumption number 4 in chapter seven **'YOU have the RIGHT to disagree or agree with any FACT or OPINION but you MUST EXPLAIN WHY'**.

FIND YOUR OWN OPINIONS

Everyone starts somewhere whether it is just agreeing with an opinion, interpretation or theory to moving to the opposite end of the scale by disagreeing and putting forward alternative opinions, interpretations and theories. The golden rule is you must explain why you formed an opinion AND your explanation must be logical.

Questions that help you find your opinion

1. Did the author express an opinion?
2. What was his/her opinion?
3. Did you agree or disagree with the author's opinion?
4. Why did you agree or disagree?
5. If you disagreed explain why?
6. Do you have an alternative opinion?
7. Explain your alternative opinion and why you hold this view?

YOUR OPINION IS IMPORTANT

Expressing your opinion or views on other people's interpretation or theories is important because it shows that you have understood the topic. Expressing your opinion shows you have evaluated what you have read. It shows that you can add something extra (your intellect) to the discussion by incorporating your own opinion, interpretation or views into your essay.

Students who can express their own thoughts will generally find their work more engaging and rewarding. Tutors love to read work where students demonstrate they are capable of thinking for themselves. They often award higher marks to those students who put their thoughts into well-constructed and logically argued essays. This additional thinking and expression sorts out the average students from the 1ST class students.

Opinions Based on Data

Opinions, interpretations or theories based on scientific data, research or published statistics are a special category. They go beyond expressing personal preferences, they are based on data. If you disagree with these and want to challenge them, you must have read and understood the data or research on which they are based. Remember if you have an alternative opinion, interpretation or argument it must have a logical explanation based on the data or research. If you express a view without having read and considered the data, your opinion will lack authority.

In the next chapter we look at when adding your ideas amounts to adding someone else's ideas. This is what we call plagiarism. In the next chapter we will look at how to avoid the humiliation and embarrassment of this allegation.

¶ Top Tip

"Great minds discuss ideas;
Average minds discuss events;
Small minds discuss people."

— Eleanor Roosevelt

CHAPTER 14
CHEATING

IN THE LAST CHAPTER we looked at the advantages of adding your own ideas to your essay, to make it more interesting and engaging. Adding your own ideas will get you higher marks for your essay - a win scenario, except when you cheat! In this chapter we look at cheating and how to avoid the humiliation and embarrassment of this allegation.

OFFICIALLY IT'S CALLED PLAGIARISM

When you set out your own views or thoughts in an essay this is great. When you steal the words of someone else and pretend they are your words this is cheating and called plagiarism. We all read other people opinions, views or interpretations in magazines, books, newspapers, blogs and online. Sometimes you want to repeat what you have read or heard and that is perfectly ok if you credit that person with their work.

USING QUOTATIONS

Let's say you read an amazing book and wanted to use the exact words in your essay. This would be ok if you made it clear, by using quotation marks ["......"] to enclose the words, sentences or paragraphs. You must also attribute the work to its author, by referring to the author either on the page or in a footnote. You must also include the work in the bibliography, which lists all the published materials you have used.

Example

Time for another example.

A friend, Snigdha, gave me a wonderful gift, a book by Dr Seuss. Dr Seuss was a famous American children's author whose books on one level are simply stories. On a deeper level his stories are about life and overcoming obstacles. Dr Seuss begins his book with the words:

"Congratulations!

Today is your day.

You're off to Great Places!"[8]

His opening pages immediately prepare the reader to expect that a great adventure is about to take place and they are not disappointed.

I have used several sentences from Dr Seuss' book so I have given the quotation a paragraph of its own. If you are intending to quote more than one or two sentences give the quotation its own paragraph enclosed within quotation

---

[8] Dr Seuss, Oh, The Places You'll Go!

marks.

You may not want to use a whole sentence or paragraph. Here you can add some of the words in your sentence but the same rules apply: use your quotation marks and attribute the work to the original author.

Example
The best feature of children's books is they take children to imaginary places with such simple phrases as: "One day George woke up to find that everything around him looked strange!"[9] Children immediately want to know what happens next.

Here I have only quoted one sentence at the end of a general discussion on the way children's books begin. The quotation marks make it clear which are the words of the original author.

Where you have very long sentences or paragraphs you may want to shorten the quotation. If you want to shorten a quotation or you want to use only part of a sentence you must indicate this by using three leader dots... (no more and no less than three dots!). The leader dots start where you shorten the quotation. Leader dots may appear at the beginning, in the middle or at the end of a sentence.

Example
"One day George woke up to find that everything around him looked strange!"

---

[9] From the imaginary story book of SuzyQ

a) I really like short phrases such as "One day…everything around him looked strange!" it takes children to the centre of the adventure in a few quick words. The leader dots are in the middle because I removed the middle part of the quotation.

b) I really like short phrases such as "…everything around him looked strange!"
The leader dots are at the beginning because I removed the beginning of the quotation.

c) I really like short phrases such as "One day…"
The leader dots are at the end because I removed the end of the quotation.

PARA-PHRASING, REWORDING OR SUMMARISING

Dealing with quotations is very easy but it is more difficult when you read someone else's work, you want to use it but don't want to quote it. When you want to reword or summarise the work you have read or heard into your own words, this is called paraphrasing. You may want to reword something because it will be shorter or a better fit for your essay. You may paraphrase a quotation, theory or podcast discussion.

You must acknowledge the original author as the person with the opinion, theory, interpretation or view but you don't need to use quotation marks. You cannot just pretend that the opinion, theory, interpretation or view you have summarised or reworded is your own work: this is plagiarism. You acknowledge the original author by either referring to him/her/or them on the page or in a footnote. You also refer to the work in the bibliography at the end of the essay.

What Happens If You Are Relying on One Reference Book, Authority or Source?

Whether you refer to published works by quoting, paraphrasing, rewording or summarising you should be careful to make a note of whether you are relying on one source for all your arguments. This should make you think about whether you have done enough research to consider a range of different views on the essay topic. If you are relying on one source are you only presenting one side of the argument? We know from our evaluation chapters that the key to getting 1ST class grades is to consider several different arguments, evaluate them and then grade them. **You should aim to research different published works that hold opposing views to get different arguments on your essay topic.** I would say that a minimum or three or four difference sources or books should be used in most essays. The more complicated the essay the more reference sources and books you will need to use.

Take a Careful Note

The key is in accurate record taking. You need to devise a system where you indicate in the margin of a page, in a diagram or on a recording;

- **the author, publication and reference pages.** When you are reading an interpretation, opinion or theory based on someone else's work you should have a clear record of the author, publication and page ref-

erence. Use the reference bibliography tool in Microsoft Office to complete this as you take notes or write your essay rather than leaving this task until the end, it saves lots of time.
- When you intend to use **quotations make sure you record them accurately.**
- When you have your **own thoughts** and views make sure that this is clear in your records.

What Happens When You Don't Take a Careful Record?

When you have read the opinions of several different authors and several commentaries it is easy to forget who said what, when or to think that something you read was your own thoughts. This is why it is so important to make a careful record of what was said and who said it. When you get confused it is easy to accidently use someone else's work as if it was your own idea.

Plagiarism Is Serious Academic Misconduct

When you attempt to steal the words, ideas or theories of other authors you become a cheat. Most schools and colleges have very strict policies on plagiarism and consider it serious misconduct. School and colleges have computer software that can process your essay and record the percentage of published material that appears in your essay. You will not fool your school or college.

Students fail to realise that published works have a style of writing that is very easy to spot and is very different from the way many students write. Students often cut and paste extracts from published works into their notes because it is easier than writing out a note. This is ok if you do not cut and paste that work into your essay without referring to the author. The published sections that are pasted into your essay have a clear and different written style to your own work and it is obvious to your tutor.

As a law tutor, I read parts of student's essays that were taken from published sources and were not properly referenced. There was a clear difference between the published style and the student's own writing style. It is difficult to change your writing style and it is easy to spot where one work ends and another author's work begins!

Assessment Essays Need to Be Your Own Work

The final stage where students sometimes fail the rules on plagiarism is where they are writing an essay for a formal assessment. The assessment rules require that the work you submit is all your own work. You cannot co-operate or collaborate with other students in preparing and writing your essay. Make sure that you do not discuss your work or share your work with other students.

When students work together they will use similar words, phrases or even make the same errors in the same places in their essays. These are all signs of co-operation or collaboration and just like the written styles of published authors they are easy to spot.

A final word of warning: sometimes when students are desperate they take, download or copy another student's essay and hand it in as their own work. Make sure you never leave your computer without logging out a password protected screen. Don't send your work to printers that you have not tested are working. You don't want your work printing out several days later for other students to pick up. Make sure when you send something to print you are at the printer to collect ALL your printed copies before someone else takes them.

Never share your storage device or allow other students to access your cloud or folders with exam essays. Always keep draft copies of your work until final examinations are formally announced. If there is a dispute you can prove that you wrote that 1ST class essay.

Consequences of Being Caught Cheating

You will not be given a grade for any work where substantial plagiarism has been found and you will have to re-write your essay. You may also have a very stern conversation with a senior professor. You should read the rules on plagiarism for your school or college very carefully. Most schools or colleges also provide guidance on how to properly reference your work; if you have any concerns read their guidance and ask for help.

Should I Get an Essay Writing Company to Write My Essay?

There are commercial companies that can provide you with an essay plan and suggested essays for your assessment. Do not be tempted to take this short cut. These essays will not help you when you sit in an examination room on your own with an assessment paper. There are no short cuts to organising your thoughts, learning how to read, evaluate and decide what you think and finally writing your 1ST class essays.

There is so much satisfaction in having done your best, produced a great essay and getting that grade.

What you learn each time you write an essay is an investment in your future that will develop your future learning, as opposed to a one-off essay purchase. Purchasing an essay will not help you the next time you are in class or a laboratory where you will have to understand the lesson without the help of your essay writer.

¶ Top Tip

Not sure
whether you should refer to the original author?
REFERENCE IT

CHAPTER 15
PLAN THAT ESSAY

YOU HAVE COMPLETED the stages of R.E.D. learning and now it is time to tie everything together into that brilliant essay. Time to start writing? NO not yet. Every good essay starts with a plan. Don't have time for a plan? - trust me on this- a good plan will make writing your essay much quicker. As the old saying goes - 'preparation, preparation, preparation...fail to prepare and prepare to fail!' In this chapter we will look at some easy essay structures to follow and how to plan an outline for your essay.

WRITE AN ESSAY PLAN

You should write an essay plan, in a style that fits your learning style. Some students will draw a map or diagram, others may have a written plan or a picture. Whatever your preferred learning style you must commit your essay plan to some physical form that you can use. Whatever method of record you choose for your essay plan it should NOT be kept in your head because once you start writing it will disappear!

USE YOUR ESSAY PLAN

Head plans often get confused, lost or worst disappear when you begin to write your essay. Record your plan and use it as a guide when you start to write or type your essay. Keep referring to your plan and check that you are not missing out any important topics as your writing progresses. Your essay plan is a tool to help you not something that you produce and then leave under your laptop or a pile of books. Use your plan. **Your plan keeps you on track and makes sure you don't miss important topics you identified in the earlier stages.**

You have done most of the hard work but there is still some thinking left to do. Having identified the key facts, topics, gaps in information and evaluated the arguments it is time to think how you are going to present this information in your essay. **A plan needs a structure** so we will look at essay structures.

PLAN A STRUCTURE FOR MY ESSAY?

Think of the structure of your essay as the frame that will support all the content you will put in your essay. **A good structure will make your essay easier to read and the arguments will appear in a logical order.** A good structure will make your essay stand out from other essays with a poor or no structure. All good essays have a good structure, just as all mammals have a backbone.

Each Essay Needs Its Own Essay Structure

There are different structures for different essays. **You must think about your essay structure in the planning stage and never simple apply the same structure to every essay.** Each essay is different from the previous one and the structure you choose will change depending on the question to be answered and the subject.

A Basic Essay Structure

A **simple structure** would have three sections:

a) **Introduction** - what is the problem I am going to discuss?

b) **Discussion** - middle section - a discussion of the issues (e.g. arguments A, B, C, & D)

c) **Conclusion** - end section - your summary and conclusion on the subject.

Advanced Essay Structures

In a more complex structure you will need to develop the basic structure. Here you need to think about introducing additional sections.

Background

No essay should start by immediately discussing the main arguments. The background introduces the context of the discussion. This section sets the scene for the discussion that will follow.

The background section is different from the introduction. The introduction says 'hello, my name is essay and today I will be discussing A topic'. The background section says, 'we are discussing A topic today because ...these factors have led to increasing problems with ...In discussing A topic we hope to look at the way that we can overcome these problems.'

Preliminary Issues

A preliminary issue is any problems you need to address before you get into the main discussion. This section may define key topics or words. It could include an interpretation or discussion of an important issue that needs to be dealt with before the main discussion. If you find you have no preliminary points, then ignore this section and move to the main discussion.

Example of a complex essay structure

i. An introduction

ii. Background

iii. Preliminary issues

iv. Discussion
Here is where you will introduce your main issues or topics for discussion in the essay in a logical order.

v. Conclusion

CHOOSE A STRUCTURE FOR YOUR MAIN DISCUSSIONS (CONTENT STRUCTURE)

In the R.E.D. learning you put your topics and arguments in order, starting with the best arguments on top. You may choose this as the content structure for your essay; we will call this **best argument on top structure**.

Another structure is to discuss arguments in the order they arise, we call this in **chronological order.** You start at the beginning or earliest event and work forward to the current time or last event. You may also use a structure where you discuss arguments by grouping them together into topics in an order that you decide, a **topic structure.**

Sometimes the essay question will suggest a content structure for you, let's call this follow the question structure. For example, if your essay question asks you to discuss three issues in a particular order that should be the structure for your essay. When you deal with each point in the order they arise in your question we call this **follow the question structure.**

Sometimes the subject may suggest an obvious content structure to tackle the essay. I call this the **subject structure.** For example, you have an essay where you are required to discuss a biological process, such as the production and development of blood cells in the human body. The logical place to start is at the beginning of the process by describing the component part of blood, how is it produced and what it does in the human body. You may then move on to discuss the system for transporting blood and how blood cells are damaged and then repaired by the human body.

In the planning stage consider at least two potential content structures. Ask yourself which structure is the easiest for the reader to follow?

- best arguments first?
- chronological order?
- topic order?
- follow the essay question?

- follow the subject?

Where Do I Put My Views and Ideas in an Essay Structure?

OK, having considered the different types of structures (essay and content structures) what have you missed out? Your ideas, your opinion, your interpretation and assessment of the issues. **You must plan where to put your ideas for each new essay.** You cannot simply put them in the same place every time. You need to choose a place that works with your essay structure, content structure, essay question and helps the reader.

There are several places to consider putting your ideas:

Beginning of Each Topic

What about having your ideas at the beginning before you discuss published views? This is probably not a great place as it is far too early and your tutor will expect you to discuss published views first.

End of Each Topic

If you are using the topic structure, it may be a good idea to put your ideas at the end of each topic after you have discussed the views of published authors. If you have several topics, then at the end of each topic, where you wish to express an alternative view or opinion, may be a good place rather than leaving all your ideas until the end of the essay.

End of The Essay

Some students prefer to put their ideas at the end of the essay just before the final conclusion. This structure can work well especially if your opinions are about predicting or commenting on future developments. Placing your ideas about future developments towards the end of the essay fits into a chronological structure.

The important task is to spend time thinking about where you are going to put your ideas and mark it out on your essay plan.

Why Bad Structures Don't Work

So now you understand why it is so important to plan how you are going to weave your essay together, adding the facts, your evaluation of published authors and your own views and opinions. If you do not plan, there is a risk that everything gets mixed up together. A confusing essay will lose marks if you do not set out your arguments in an easy to follow essay structure. A confusing structure will mean that all the good work you have done in preparing, reading, thinking and evaluating will not be obvious to the tutor. You are wasting valuable marks.

Spend More Time Writing About the Important Topics or Problems (Weighting)

The last but important decision is deciding where you spend most time writing in your essay. The general rule is that the more important, complex or central to your main discussion the more time you should spending writing about these topics. These topics will also occupy the most space in your essay.

I often had to read assessment essays where students clearly had not thought about their essay plan. They wrote too much on introductory or background issues and then very little on the real problems that they needed to write about. These essays lost valuable marks because they simply didn't have enough detail in the right places in their essays. Students don't get marks for writing the right length of essay otherwise everyone who handed in their 3,000-word essay would get a great mark. **Students get 1ST class marks for writing about the right topics with the right amount of details.**

Weighting Extended Essays

Extended essays are more complicated and longer than short essays. You will need a slightly different approach. You are likely to have chapters in your extended essay so decide the order of your chapters. Decide where you will place your key chapters in the essay structure. When you prepare your extended essay plan you may have three or four key chapters. Your key issues should be distributed mainly throughout these key chapters. These are the chapters where you will spend more time writing.

ESSAYS WITH WORD LIMITS

If your essay has a word limit you should avoid going over the limit as there are usually penalties for doing this. You will want to maximize your essay marks so you should not write an essay that is significantly less than your word limit. For example, if you are asked to write an essay not exceeding 3,000 words you should NOT write an essay of 1,000 words. In a significantly shorter essay the chances are you have missed out some important information.

Having done your research and written on your topic don't try to write more just to get within one or two words of the word limit. All you will do is repeat what you have already said and this will not get you extra marks. For example, if you have a 3,000-word limit. You have written 2,500 words and have fully dealt with the essay question then stop writing!

An Overview on Planning, Structure and Weighting

You must decide and plan where the most important and complex issues are in your essay. Make sure that you give these complex or important areas the most detail and space in your essay. This will mean that you take the reader to the core of your arguments and spend the most time at the right places. **Tutors are more inclined to mark work highly when it has been well planned, structured and has the right amount of detail in the right areas, so plan it out before writing your essay.**

Conclusions

Summarise and Conclude at the End of Each Main Topic

Think of playing rounders or baseball at school – the object is to get around the pitch touching in at each base until you get to the end. You want to make sure that the tutor has a summary and conclusion at the end of each main topic, like you are touching base as you move around the pitch. At last base you will have your final conclusion.

If you have summarised and concluded, at the end of each main topic your tutor will understand your reasoning and decisions. When the tutor has been carefully led through your essay to the final conclusion you have accomplished one of the main features of a 1ST class essay: a clear and logical structure. You are also more likely to convince your tutor that your arguments, opinions and supporting information present a convincing and well-argued essay.

A Final Conclusion

Well the good news is there is always a final conclusion at the end of an essay. Remember this is not a repetition of your discussion in the main body of the essay; it is a brief summary with a final conclusion that answers the essay question. Your tutor should clearly understand your position having read the conclusion. When you have written the final conclusion test it out, read it. Does it sum up concisely?

A Consistent Final Conclusion

The final conclusion should not be a surprise. Your arguments or discussion in the main body of the essay should be consistent with the arguments and evaluations you have made earlier in your essay.

SEVEN important questions you should ask when recording your essay plan:

1. **What structure should I use for my essay?**

2. **What should I put in the background section?**

3. Do I have any **preliminary issues** that I need to deal with first?

4. **What structure should I use for my content?**

   - best arguments first?
   - chronological order?
   - topic order?
   - follow the essay question structure?
   - follow the subject structure?

5. **Where will I put my own ideas** in this essay?

6. **Where will I spend more time writing (weighting)?**

7. What are my **conclusions** on each **main topic** and **final conclusion?**

¶ TOP TIP

Preparation, Preparation, Preparation
"You're off to Great Places!"[10]

[10] Dr Seuss Oh, The Places You'll Go

Chapter 16

How to Write a 1st Class Essay

A clear logical structure is the best way of showing off the great reading, thinking and evaluating you have already done. If you can also write your essay in a style that is easy to read, your work should get great scores.

Your writing style is the way you communicate your ideas, arguments, interpretation and opinions. To communicate your thoughts clearly it is important that your work is easy to read. When you say what you mean, keep it simple and write in a formal style - the job is almost done. Writing a 1st class essay starts with clearly communicating with the reader.

SAY WHAT YOU MEAN & KEEP IT SIMPLE

The most important thing to remember is that you should write clearly so your meaning is easily understood. Avoid writing anything that is confusing, vague, unclear or simply fails to communicate what you mean. The easiest way of doing this is to say exactly what you mean and keep it simple. This means finding a balance between not being too brief and leaving out the details and writing too much. When you over-use language the words get in the way of your message and stops the reader from focusing on the meaning.

An advantage of saying what you mean and keeping it simple is that it will keep you on topic. The more you elaborate the more likely it is that you will start to go off the main topic into unnecessary or irrelevant areas. Do you have friends who just can't get to the point in a conversation? How hard and frustrating is it when you just want to know the point of the very long story?

HOW TO FIND THE RIGHT WRITING STYLE FOR AN ESSAY?

You understand the importance of saying what you mean and keeping it simple but you also should remember to write in a style that is appropriate for an essay. Try to think of your writing style as the way you would speak to a person if you were having a conversation.

Informal Writing

Think of the sort of language you would use if you were texting a friend, it would be informal. The sentences may be incomplete. You may use abbreviations or words that have a special meaning between you and your friends rather than their literal meaning. Your style may communicate your personality or feelings, such as emojis or other icons. You may include jokes and punctuations that reflect your mood such as capital letters or exclamation marks.

Informal writing is NEVER acceptable in essays. You must try very hard not to slip into this style of writing. Would you write to your friends in the same style you would write to your boss or manager at work? No! I have written this book in informal language because the main purpose is to help you read and understand how to write 1ST class essays with ease. You will have plenty of time to read formal books for your essay research.

Formal Writing

Essays require a formal style of writing. Think of the style of reports and books written by professors, lawyers, experts, academics and published authors. **You need to write your essay with a formal style of writing so it is time to put on your best voice!** Your best voice does not mean a pompous voice with lots of unnecessary old-fashioned words. **Think of this voice as a modern, polite and professional voice.**

- You should write in complete sentences.
- You should choose the correct words and terminology for your subject.
- You should use standard grammar and
- You should use the correct spelling for words.

Let's recap:

✓ Say what you mean

- ✓ Keep it simple
- ✓ Write in a formal style

FOLLOW THE RULES – GRAMMAR AND SPELLING

Your final challenge is to make sure that you follow the basic rules of grammar and spelling because this will allow your tutor to understand the meaning of your words quickly. Poor punctuation, grammar and spelling requires your tutor to re-read your work to understand its intended meaning. The more your tutor must stop and re-read, the more distracted they are from what you are trying to say in your essay.

Imagine you are having a conversation with a friend. You are opposite each other and she/he is telling you something serious that you need to hear. Behind your friend and in your eyesight is someone jumping up and down and waving at you. You are trying to listen to your friend but the person behind her/him is distracting you. Poor grammar just gets in the way of reading the interesting content you are writing; this is why it is important to spend time getting the grammar and spelling right.

GET THE GRAMMAR RIGHT

A short recap of some basic rules of grammar.

- **The sentence.**
  A sentence always starts with a capital letter and usually ends with a full stop. If your sentence ends with a question, always end the sentence with a question mark (?). There must be a subject, a person or thing, which is the focus of the sentence (called a

noun). There must be a verb which is a word that expresses action or an occurrence.

e.g. The goal-keeper saved the ball from hitting the goal.

In this example 'the goal-keeper' is the noun and his action 'saved' is the verb.
Sentences are the essential base of your writing. Sentences can vary in length. There are short and long sentences. The rules on constructing sentences become more complicated the longer the sentence. **If you are not familiar with advanced rules of grammar just say what you mean and keep it short.**

- **Paragraphs-**
  These are groups of sentences on the same topic or issue. Paragraphs help the reader to break up the text into topics that they can read more easily and quickly. The key rule is that **one issue = one paragraph**. When checking your work look for very long paragraphs. Ask: have I dealt with more than one issue in this paragraph? If you have dealt with more than one issue start a new paragraph where you start to deal with the new issue.

  A paragraph should be more than one sentence. If you find one sentence on its own in a paragraph, ask whether it belongs to the paragraph above or below its position.

  Long paragraphs are more difficult to read than shorter paragraphs. It is easier to read paragraphs of varying sizes rather than paragraphs that are all the same length. Vary the size of your paragraphs if you find they are all the same length by adding a bit more or taking out something irrelevant. When checking your work look for very long paragraphs and break them up. You should never have a paragraph that is the whole length of a page. A paragraph size will depend on your topic and will generally be about four or five sentences.

- **Commas [,]**

  These little symbols help to punctuates sentences. Never use a comma before the word 'and'. They help to separate the main part of the sentence from a sub-clause (a part of the sentence).

  Example

  'the ball shot past the goal-keeper, despite his best efforts to stop it'.

  The main sentence is 'the ball shot past the goal-keeper'; the sub-clause is 'despite his best efforts to stop it.'

  Commas also separate qualifying words.

  Example

  'However, despite a great goal, the goal-keeper performed very well.'

  Commas are also used to separate items in a list.

Example
You should read, evaluate, decide, plan and then write a 1ST class essay.

- **Quotation marks ['...']**
Short quotations of one or two sentences can be incorporated into a sentence using quotations marks at the beginning and end of the quotation. A quotation of more than one or two sentences should start on a new line after a colon [:].

Example
Hayley wrote in her diary:
'I would never forget that long summer day in 2017 when my life would change forever. It was a long, happy day of yellow sunshine.'
If you are not quoting a complete sentence or only part of a quotation, then you should introduce the quotation with **three** leader dots [...]

- **Semi-colon [;]**
The semi-colon joins two parts of a sentence that could be linked or separated with a full stop.

Example
Harry was annoyed with P J; he had been rude and offensive to his friend, Monica.
The same sentence could be written as two short sentences.
Harry was annoyed with PJ. He had been rude and offensive to his friend, Monica.

- **Colon [:]**
  A colon is used to set up a quotation, to introduce a list of items or to define or expand a statement.

  Examples

  - Marta tells Giovanni in her poem: 'I will not follow you now or at any other time.'
  - Marta collected her things: her shoes, bags, winter scarf, hat and coat.
  - Marta's coat was brightly embroidered with yellow, blue and green birds: nightingales in full flight.

You should always use a dictionary or a grammar reference book (or use an online version) to check the rules. When you are unsure don't just guess. The rules of grammar and spelling are not always logical! Have a look at appendix C for recommended reference books and websites.

SPELLING - GET IT RIGHT

Tutors hate reading poor spelling because it slows down their reading and understanding of the work. Poor spelling means the tutor must spend time guessing what the word should be or re-reading the work to try and understand the intended meaning.

There are two main reason students misspell words. First they write a word that is similar to the word that they intended to use. For example, the sentence may have required the word drawn and instead they accidently write or type the word lawn. The spell checker will not recognise this as a misspelling (as lawn is correctly spelt). Sometimes the correct spelling of a word depends on the meaning and context of the sentence. Common examples where the spell checker will not help you are with the words: lose/loose, your/ you're, their/there.

The second situation where words are misspelled is because students fail to apply a spell checker AND check their final version. I know that sometime deadlines are tight but having done all that good work it seems such a waste of easy marks not to make sure your work is presented at its best.

Always Apply a Spell Checker to Your Final Work and Then YOU Need to Check It for Mistakes

- Check for missing words that have not been added to the sentence.

- Find words that for some freaky reason the spell checker did not find.

- Spot those words that the auto-correcting or predictive text spelling function on your laptop changed to a word you did not want to use.

- Check to see if words have more than one way of spelling them. There is often a difference between spelling the same words in the USA and UK.

- Remember names and laces will not always be discovered by a spell checker. Did you spot the spelling error in the last sentence? laces instead of places!

BEST TIME FOR CHECKING?

I find that the best time to check my work is in the morning when my mind is fresh. Try to write your essay or chapters for your extended essay and then leave them for at least 24 hours. Your mind needs the time to forget what you thought you wrote and to see what you actually wrote.

Go back to your work after a day or two and check for spelling and grammar errors. Find a quiet café, park or somewhere in the library on a comfortable chair and read your work carefully.

The worst time to check your work is when you are under pressure from a deadline or tired. Too many students check their essays as they stand in line to hand in their assessment essays and it looked perfect until they get their grade.

READY TO COMPLETE THAT ESSAY

When planning and writing your essay you will:

- ✓ Apply R.E.D. - Read. Evaluate. Decide.
- ✓ Plan your structure.
- ✓ Spend more time on the important main topics or problems - weighting.
- ✓ Write - say what you mean & keep it simple.
- ✓ Write – stay on topic.
- ✓ Write in a formal style.
- ✓ Check your grammar and spelling.

¶ TOP TIP

Learn from the mistakes of others..."

– Eleanor Roosevelt

CHAPTER 17
CONCLUSION

"Be the change that you wish to see in the world."

– MAHATMA GANDHI

THE PURPOSE OF THIS BOOK is to help you think, organise and write 1ST class essays. Follow these simple rules and I promise that you will find the task of planning, organising and writing much easier. You have the task of reading the books on your chosen academic subjects and putting in the hard work.

When you start using R.E.D. learning you will get quicker and better at applying these simple steps. You will spend MORE time thinking and evaluating. You will find your own views, opinions and interpretations. Be confident and listen to your inner voice. You have the right to express your own views and opinions. When you have completed your first essay using R.E.D. learning you will feel great - CONGRATULATIONS! This is a system of study that will help you today and in the future.

Your essays are the way you will show that you have:

- **understood** your academic subjects
- the **skills** to critically assess information
- the **ability** to present information in a format that is intelligent, logical and persuasive
- the **intelligence** for independent thinking

As you develop so will your abilities to read, evaluate and make important decisions.

Your essays are the way that you will achieve your dreams by obtaining the qualifications that you need to embark on your chosen career. Dream it, Plan it, Do it, can you see your future? The right study skills will help you to achieve your full potential. I hope you will join me on the next step of the journey. If you plan to write a dissertation my next book will help you plan and organise. Visit my website **www.inspiredtostudy.org** to find further study skills books, resources, webinars and workshops that you can attend.

Study skills for students is the first part of your development. As you embark on a professional career you will develop work and life skills to take you to further dreams.

People have over thousands of years used their skills to survive, develop and adapt. Your study, work and life skills are the culmination of human development over millions of years. I wish you an epic journey into that future and leave you with the words of an amazing human being, Mr. Nelson Mandela:

"Education is the most powerful weapon you can use to change the world."

– NELSON MANDELA

APPENDICES

Appendix A - 5 Stages of Essay Writing

Appendix B - How to Work Out Time Estimates

Appendix C - Recommended further reading for grammar and spelling

Appendix D - Recipe Blog

APPENDIX A - 5 STAGES OF ESSAY WRITING

THE 5 STAGES OF OPINION WRITING	
STAGE 1	Start - **read** your instructions
STAGE 2	main **research** and reading
STAGE 3	**Thinking and planning**
STAGE 4	**writing** your essay
STAGE 5	**check** that essay

Stage 1: Read your instructions

You should read your essay instructions, background information and any diagrams, maps or timelines you have been provided. Read the information about the deadline for submission (record the time and date carefully) and any rules or guidance for completing the task.

Think of this first stage as a warm up session at the gym, stretching before a football game or the first 15 minutes when you get into the swimming pool.

Stage 2: Main research and detail reading

This is the detailed research and reading on your subject. Do your main research and reading which will form the main content of your essay. This is complex reading that will take the longest time and requires the most focus. This is when you are so engrossed in reading you forget all about your phone, social media or texting your friends.

Stage 3: Thinking and planning

There is no point in research and reading if you do not have time to think about what you have read and time to plan what you are going to write. At this stage you should complete an essay plan.

Stage 4: Writing your essay

The time this takes will depend on how quickly you type or write, the length of the essay and how well you have planned at stage three. At this stage don't include time for editing, checking or minor structural changes to your essay.

Stage 5: Time to check your work

This is the time to check your essay, edit and carry out any minor structural changes. Run the spell checker AND re-read the essay for spelling and grammar errors not picked up by the spell checker. No work is complete until it has been properly checked twice!

Remember visit **www.inspiredtostudy.org** to download your FREE infographics.

APPENDIX B – HOW TO WORK OUT A TIME ESTIMATE

Stage 1. - Guess the time you need to read the introductory materials

Stage 2. - Guess the time you need to spend on your main research and reading.

Stage 3. - Thinking and planning.

Stage 4. - Writing your essay.

Stage 5. - Checking your essay.

REMEMBER you need to have time for BREAKS, LUNCH AND DINNER so add in periods for your breaks at stages that YOU find convenient.

ADD UP YOUR TIME

Time to add up the time you have estimated for stages 1 - 5 if you intend to complete the work in one go. If you intend to check your work later then add up the time for the tasks under stages 1 - 4.

You will get better at judging the time for the five stages the more you use this system. It is important that you **make sure you have the time to complete the work you have planned** or re-think your schedule. You can break up the time to fit each stage if you plan your work over several days as long as they are kept in the same order.

SET YOUR TIMER & BEGIN

Set a timer on your watch, phone or PC for the time you have allowed for stage one. Now put the timer out of sight and start to complete the work. When the timer goes off have you completed the task? If you have not completed the task guess how much longer you need, re-set the timer and put it out of sight and return to your work. Once you have completed stage one, set the timer for stage two and move on until you get to stage five.

EXAMPLE TIME ESTIMATE

Stage	Task	Time estimate
1	Reading instructions	15 mins
2	Research and detail reading	180 min
3	Thinking and planning	45 mins
4	Writing	60 mins
5	Checking	30 mins
	Total time	330 mins (5 hours 30 mins)

REMEMBER:

1. You need to add in break times, they often fit in at the end of one of the stages or after about 30-45 minutes of study. Having regular and short rest breaks is key to keeping your mind alert and active.
2. You can complete your work over several days. Try to finish a stage before taking a break for a day or more. You will find that when you start the new stage the following day(s) later you will need to re-read your earlier work to get up to speed with your previous thoughts and work.
3. A plan over 3 days may look like this:

EXAMPLE of a TIME ESTIMATE PLAN over 3 days

Stage	Task	Time estimate
1	Reading instructions	15 mins
2	Research and reading	180 min
Day 1		**3 hours 15 mins**
3	Thinking and planning	45 mins
Day 2		**45 mins**
4	Writing	60 mins
5	Checking	30 mins
Day 3		**90 mins**
3 days	**Total time**	**5 hours 30 mins**

EXAMPLE of a TIME ESTIMATE PLAN for an assessment

3 hours with 3 essay questions to complete

You will have already:

- completed your revision
- **Practised previous assessment questions** provided by your university or college
- You may have **prepared your own blank generic essay plan**

Time plan	Stage	Task	Time estimate
09.00	1	Read –your assessment papers and select your 3 essay questions.	15 mins
	2	Re-read your selected essay questions.	
9.15	3	Thinking and planning (15 mins each essay)	45 mins
10.00	4	Writing (35 mins each essay)	1 hr 45 min
11.45	5	Checking (5 mins each essay)	15 mins
12.00		**Total time**	**3 hours**

- Remember in assessments conditions you need to **pay attention to the time - it progresses really fast!** There is no point in 1ST-class reading, evaluation and decisions if you do not leave sufficient time to WRITE and CHECK your essay.

- **Practice at least 3 timed-essays** under assessment conditions **BEFORE the final assessment** this will help you work out YOUR Time Plan and help you manage your time in the real assessment.

- **Have a Time Plan** that works for YOU - record the actual time you need to start the key stages and have it in front of you. The plan above assumes the assessment starts at 9.00am and finishes at 12.00pm. As you hit your time markers finish your stage within the next 5 minutes and move on to the next section so you stay on track.

- Cover your averages. If you have 3 essays to write make sure that you complete each essay. It is easier to get a higher average grade by completing 3 essays reasonably well rather than writing 2 brilliant essays but failing to attempt the 3rd essay.

- Remember you cannot use a timer or device that makes a sound during the assessment.

Visit **www.inspiredtostudy.org** to download your FREE infographics.

Appendix C- Recommended Reading for Grammar and Spelling

Dictionary

Little Oxford English Dictionary, University Press or online at

http://www.oxforddictionaries.com/definition/english/online

http://www.collinsdictionary.com/english-thesaurus

Grammar reference

http://learnenglish.britishcouncil.org/en/quick-grammar

http://www.bbc.co.uk/skillswise/topic-group/sentence-grammar

Reference

Oxford Thesaurus of English, University Press or online at

http://www.oxforddictionaries.com/thesaurus/

Visit **www.inspiredtostudy.org** to download your FREE infographics.

Appendix D – Recipe Blog

Do you want some help with easy to follow healthy food recipes? Go to Snig's Kitchen for a celebration of food from around the world, recipes, cooking tips and reviews

http://snigskitchen.blogspot.co.uk/

BIBLIOGRAPHY

Retrieved from Oxforddictionaries.com: http://www.oxforddictionaries.com (January 2016)

Department of Health. (2004). *At least five a week.* London.

Fry Ketteridge and Marshall. (2003). *A Handbook for Teaching and Learning in Higher Education.* London: Kogan Page.

NHS direct. (2015, July 11). NHS.uk. Retrieved from http://www.nhs.uk/Livewell/fitness/Pages/physical-activity-guidelines-for-adults.aspx.

Oppezzo, M., & L, S. D. (2014 July). Learning, Memory and Cognition. *Journal of Experimental Psychology vol 40* (4), 1142-1152.

Seuss, D. (2003). *Oh, The Places You'll Go!* London: HarperCollinsChildren's Book.

Stevenson. (2002). Little Oxford English Dictionary. Oxford: Oxford University Press.

About the Author

Suzanne Reece is an education coach. She is a solicitor (currently non- practising) who worked in legal firms for over 17 years. She later moved into education teaching post graduate law at City, University of London for nearly 10 years. Critical to her role were skills teaching, course design and assessments. Suzanne also supervised LLM dissertation students, delivered academic support and provided study coaching to post -graduates students.

Early in her education career it became apparent that good students were not achieving the grades they deserved. Suzanne discovered that for some students their poor study skills prevented their academic knowledge being communicated to their tutors in the right form. With the right study skills Suzanne believes that students can remove these obstacles and achieve their full potential. Her passion is helping students achieve first class grades.

Suzanne has taught thousands of students and helped them obtain first class grades. In 2015, she established Inspired to Study Ltd to provide bespoke educational skills training. Suzanne provides personal coaching and mentoring. She runs regular webinars, workshops and attends speaking events. To find our more visit, www.inspiredtostudy.org

Suzanne Reece
The Study Coach
Education Coach, Lecturer & Author

www.inspiredtostudy.org

ACKNOWLEDGEMENTS

I wish to thank everyone that has encouraged, supported and helped me in this project.

Special thanks to my brother and sister, Arlon and Deborah Reece, for their love.

To Sian, Gillian and Hayley for their impressive work in carefully editing the book. To Rachel and Sharon for being the first reviewers and for their feedback.

To all those who gave helpful suggestions, support and encouragement: Sammy Blindell, Paul Brooks, Hayley Brown, Paula Edwards, Miles Fryer, George Georgiou, Shirley Harper, Sian Lewis, Ian Martin, Sharon Neville, Rachel Oriba, Deborah Reece, Hazel Rosemin, Peter Rosemin, Marcia Scott, Surinder Tamne, Gillian Woodworth, Teresha Young.

Special thanks to Ella Brown for making the most beautiful happy drawings that adorned my office as I worked and for encouraging me to become a famous author!

To my law students at City, University of London who showed me the need to write this book and for the privilege of sharing their many achievements.

Internal formatting and arrangement by Chad Robertson www.writingnights.org

Book covers designed by Vanessa Mendozzi, Graphic designer, www.vanessamendozzidesign.com

Printed in Great Britain
by Amazon